THE ALL FEELINGS WELCOME WORKBOOK

HANDS-ON ACTIVITIES FOR PARENTS TO DEVELOP CARING, CONFIDENT, AND RESILIENT KIDS

Kelly Oriard
Callie Christensen

JB JOSSEY-BASS™
A Wiley Brand

Published by John Wiley & Sons, Inc., Hoboken, New Jersey.

ISBNs: 9781394313792 (paperback), 9781394313808 (ePub), 9781394313815 (ePDF)

Library of Congress Control Number is Available:

Cover Design: Wiley
Cover Image: © ALICIA BOCK/Stocksy/stock.adobe.com
Author Photo: © Filipe Lara

Praise for *All Feelings Welcome*

"As a child psychiatrist and advocate for children's mental health, I am deeply impressed by Kelly and Callie's book on parenting. This book is a treasure trove of wisdom, blending therapeutic principles with practical strategies that empower parents to support their children's emotional development from the earliest stages. I appreciate how this book, written by authors with a deep understanding of child development, addresses common parenting challenges and provides a roadmap for fostering a child's self-esteem, resilience, and empathy. This expertise shines through in every chapter, making this a must-read for anyone looking to nurture their child's emotional well-being. Kelly and Callie have created a unique and valuable resource that will positively impact families everywhere. I highly recommend this book to parents, caregivers, and educators seeking to create a nurturing and emotionally supportive environment for children."

–**Helen Egger**, *MD., Co-founder and Chief Medical & Scientific Officer at Little Otter,* www.littleotterhealth.com

"*All Feelings Welcome* is the parenting book that we need today! It provides you with the tools that you need to feel empowered and to take an active role in helping guide your children gain the confidence they need to navigate life and all the emotions that come along with it. I can't wait to share this book with my mom friends and colleagues and also recommend it to clients."

–**Rachel L. Goldman**, *PhD, FTOS, FASMBS-IH, licensed psychologist, speaker, and Clinical Assistant Professor in the Department of Psychiatry at NYU Grossman School of Medicine*

"All I've ever wanted as a parent is to be the best support system to my child so that they can fully grow into the person they were meant to be. With *All Feelings Welcome*, Kelly and Callie have given us a treasure trove of ways to help our kids embrace and develop their emotional well-being, and maybe even do a bit of healing ourselves along the way! This is an incredibly empowering read for anyone on their parenting journey."

–**Jason Ritter**, *actor and voice of Fox's Dad on the Emmy-nominated Apple TV+ series Slumberkins*

"*All Feelings Welcome* is a must-have book for all parents and caregivers! Kelly and Callie have crafted the ultimate practical, empowering tool to help you build and support healthy emotional well-being with your children and caregivers. You can't go wrong with this wonderful offering from the creators behind the lovable Slumberkins brand."

–**Yvette Nicole Brown**, *actress and Slumberkins superfan*

"This book is what I wanted for all the parents whose kids went to school with my kids. This book makes me hopeful for parents and caregivers and humans so when their kids experience any kind of emotions, they can guide them (and themselves) through the feelings, navigating and embracing all the scary, underwhelming, and overwhelming things life throws at them. I wish this book was published 20 years ago. Or 50 years ago. . . ."

–**Pamela Adlon**, *voice of Fox's Mom on the Emmy-nominated Apple TV+ series Slumberkins*

"*All Feelings Welcome* is a must-have book for parents and caregivers looking to support emotional resilience in their kids. Practical, inspiring, and easy to implement, the strategies in this book will help you and your kids build positive connections wherever life takes you. *All Feelings Welcome* is truly a book everyone needs to read!"

–**Allie Szczecinski**, *MSEd, Founder of Miss Behavior*

"This is an indispensable goldmine for parents! *All Feelings Welcome* leads us down the path to emotional resilience, demonstrating the ways we can best help our kids face whatever life throws their way in a confident, capable manner. The creators of Slumberkins have outdone themselves with the clear, actionable strategies in this book. Every parent needs this book! "

–**Jon Gustin**, *The Tired Dad*

"A comprehensive and compelling immersion in your child's emotional and social development, the founders of Slumberkins have created a wonderful resource for parents, teachers, and other adults who care so deeply for children. In this accessible and clear compendium is a set of insights and suggestions that will enhance the well-being of every child fortunate to have a caregiver so powerfully prepared to help them cultivate resilience and well-being in their growing lives."

–**Daniel J. Siegel**, *MD.,*
New York Times *bestselling author or co-author, The Whole Brain Child; Parenting from the Inside Out; The Power of Showing Up; The Develop*ing Mind

"In All Feelings Welcome, caregiver readers are gifted with a beautiful and well-researched guide from two caregivers/educators illuminating the path toward understanding and nurturing the emotional bond within caregiver-child dyads. As a pioneering psychologist, avid meditator, and champion for the emotional well-being of diverse youth and families, I passionately endorse this work, reminding everyone that 'People from all backgrounds deserve to access the full range of their emotions always,' a principle that shines through every page of this beautiful and important book."

–**Dr. Alfiee Breland-Noble**,
pioneering psychologist, author, Founder of mental health nonprofit The AAKOMA Project and host of the mental health podcast "Couched in Color with Dr. Alfiee."

To Aidan, Oliver, Logan, Henry, Owen, and Cora:

You are the heartbeat of this work. Every page, every reflection, every story we tell is rooted in our love for you.

We are the cycle-breaking parents because of you. You remind us daily that we can choose a new way forward—one built on connection, compassion, and the courage to grow. We may not get it right every time, but we promise to keep trying, to repair when we stumble, and to love you with everything we have.

May you always know that your feelings are welcome, that your voices matter, and that you are seen, heard, and cherished exactly as you are.

With all our love.

Contents

Introduction

Hey there. Welcome to the Workbook!

Before we dive into exercises, journal prompts, and some good old-fashioned self-reflection, we wanted to take a second to talk directly to *you*. Yes, *you*–the parent, caregiver, or grownup human who picked up this workbook and decided, "Okay, let's figure this out."

First of all, bravo. You could be doomscrolling or folding that mountain of laundry (again), but instead you're here, choosing growth. That's a big deal.

We created this workbook as a companion to *All Feelings Welcome*, and it's really about helping you take what you've read and turn it into something *lived*. Not just for your child's growth–but for yours too.

This Workbook Is About You First

Wait, what? A parenting workbook that starts with *me*?

Yep. That's the twist.

We know it can feel like parenting is 90% trying to get your kid to put on socks. But beneath that surface-level chaos is a deeper opportunity. Every time you get overwhelmed, feel stuck, or hear your own parents' voices come out of your mouth (you know the ones), it's a chance to notice what's actually driving your reactions.

That's why the first few chapters in this workbook are all about looking inward. Your core beliefs. Your patterns. The stuff that got baked in way back when you were the one being parented.

Because here's the truth: You can't build something new if you're still running on an outdated blueprint. And the coolest part? You get to rework the blueprint, starting now.

This Work Is Tender (and Kinda Weird Sometimes)

Heads up. Some of these questions might make you think, "Whoa. I did *not* expect to cry before 9 a.m. on a Tuesday." That's normal.

Other times, you might read a prompt and think, "Hmm . . . gonna skip that one and come back to it later, maybe . . . or never." Also normal.

This work isn't about doing it perfectly. It's about showing up, being honest with yourself, and knowing it's okay to feel a little messy. In fact, it means you're doing it right.

Don't Worry, You're Not Alone

We're not hovering over your shoulder, whispering, "You missed a journaling prompt." We're in this with you, stumbling through bedtime routines and snack negotiations and moments of "Did I just yell at a toddler for acting like…a toddler?"

This workbook is here to meet you wherever you are—on your best day, your roughest one, and every half-finished coffee in between.

So be gentle with yourself. Laugh when you can. Cry when you need to. And trust that every time you pause to reflect instead of react, you're doing something powerful. You're changing the story. For you and your kid.

Okay, Let's Go

You're here, and that means something. Not everyone chooses to do this kind of work, but you did. And we're really glad to be alongside you as you do.

Let's get into it.

With you,
Callie + Kelly

CHAPTER 1

Understanding Your Core Beliefs

Looking Inward to Grow Together

Parenting opens the door to one of life's most vulnerable and transformative experiences. Parenting requires us to be present with love and intention while many times lacking specific instructions. The content of this chapter starts with self-exploration before focusing on your child.

The approach in *All Feelings Welcome* begins with introspection. We examine the foundational beliefs we hold, which include deeply ingrained perceptions about ourselves and others that originate from early childhood and persistently affect our behavior despite remaining out of our awareness. Our subconscious beliefs shape our responses to our child's tears and challenges and determine how we provide them comfort. Our core beliefs become audible whispers when we experience feelings of being overwhelmed or triggered.

This workbook chapter invites you to take a moment to recognize those subtle messages.

Whether or not you've read the book, know this: Your beliefs stem from a different time and different circumstances, but you are not alone in this experience. While certain beliefs give parents strength, others burden them with unnecessary stress in their parenting roles. By approaching our past experiences with curiosity instead of criticism, we open ourselves up to healing and growth. We break away from old patterns to discover new opportunities that benefit both ourselves and our children.

Why Core Beliefs Matter in Parenting

The Connect-to-Grow approach believes our parental connections to our children stem from our own self-connection. Our self-awareness becomes filtered by the fundamental beliefs we hold.

Holding the belief that you must handle everything alone can cause burnout because you experience guilt when seeking assistance. The core belief "I'm only lovable when I'm calm and composed" manifests as shame when you become impatient. These aren't flaws—they're old survival strategies. And here, we're not judging them. Right now, we want to learn about how these patterns appear in our current lives.

When you start reading this chapter, you will probably find childhood memories rising to the surface. This is normal. This work is tender. But it's also empowering, because with awareness comes choice.

WHAT ARE CORE BELIEFS?

Core beliefs are deeply held understandings about ourselves, others, and the world. They develop in childhood based on lived experiences and shape how we interpret situations.

How they form:
- Children create stories to make sense of their world, often in black-and-white terms.
- These stories become ingrained beliefs that persist into adulthood.
- Many adults are unaware of these beliefs, but they guide behavior, emotions, and relationships.

Why they matter for parenting:
- If a parent believes "I have to be in control to feel safe," they may struggle to let their child take risks.
- If a parent believes "I am not enough," they may feel pressure to be a perfect parent.
- Identifying and challenging these beliefs allows for more conscious, connected parenting.

COMMON NEGATIVE CORE BELIEFS THAT AFFECT PARENTING
Beliefs often fall into these five categories:

CORE BELIEF AREA	EXAMPLE NEGATIVE BELIEF	HOW IT MIGHT SHOW UP IN PARENTING
SAFETY & VULNERABILITY	"The world is dangerous."	Overprotectiveness, excessive worry about child's safety.
CONTROL & CHOICE	"I have to be in control."	Struggles to let child make choices, fear of unpredictability.
WORTHINESS & LOVABILITY	"I am not enough."	Perfectionism, overcompensating as a parent.
GUILT & SHAME	"I am responsible for others' happiness."	Over-functioning, difficulty setting boundaries.
RESPONSIBILITY & SURVIVAL	"I have to handle everything alone."	Burnout, reluctance to ask for support.

Personal Reflection Activity: Uncovering Your Own Core Beliefs

Journaling prompts:

- What messages did I receive about emotions as a child?
- How was I taught to handle mistakes?
- What were the spoken and unspoken "rules" in my family about love, success, and failure?
- When my child struggles with emotions, what fears or reactions come up for me?
- Do I ever hear my parents' voices in my head when I parent? What do they say?

Uncovering Your Core Beliefs

Instead of a heavy self-examination, try **The Parenting Time Machine** game:

Step 1: Imagine Yourself as a Seven-Year-Old

- Close your eyes and picture yourself at age seven. What were you like? What made you happy, scared, or excited?
- Imagine a typical day in your childhood. Who were the adults around you? What messages did you hear?

Reflection question:

Write down three things you remember most about how adults responded to your emotions or behaviors.

Step 2: Fast-Forward to Today

- Think about how you respond when your child cries, makes a mistake, or challenges you.
- Do you hear echoes of the past? Are you repeating patterns, or breaking them?

Reflection question:

What is one thing you want to do differently for your child that you wish had been different for you?

Rewriting the Narrative: Shifting Negative Core Beliefs

Challenge:

- Choose one negative core belief you uncovered, and let's find a way to become aware of when it is driving your behavior and work to shift it to a more adaptive belief that is more true for you now.

Example:

Old Belief: *"I have to be a perfect parent or I'll fail my child."*
New Belief: *"Good enough is enough. My love and presence are what truly matter."*

Affirmation writing:

- Create a **new affirmation** that challenges an old belief. We use them all through-out as personal mantras that help ground us when we are facing a moment that brings up a negative belief we have.

Example:

"*I messed up. This is going to have a lasting impact, and it's all my fault.*"
Gently remind yourself and lean into a positive mantra, like "*I am learning and growing alongside my child. Mistakes help us connect.*"

Reflection questions:

- What is one thing I want to do differently now that I see this belief?
- How can I show my child a new, healthier way of thinking?

CHAPTER 2

Routines: Core Beliefs and Balance

Refer to CHAPTER 6 of All Feelings Welcome *for deeper learning and understanding about this concept.*

Finding Balance Through Rhythm

Before we talk about what routines should look like in your home, let's talk about what they feel like—because for children, routines aren't just about what happens next. They're about whether the world feels safe, predictable, and manageable.

In *All Feelings Welcome*, we explore how structure supports not just behavior, but emotional security. When children know what to expect, they can relax into their environment. When they have opportunities to participate in that structure— choosing their snack, picking their pajamas, brushing their teeth "all by myself"— they also build confidence in their ability to navigate the world.

As caregivers, our own beliefs about structure are shaped by how we were raised. Maybe you grew up in a home where the schedule was strict and the rules were unbendable. Maybe routines were more like loose suggestions—or didn't exist at all. Either way, those early experiences likely shaped your own core beliefs around control, flexibility, and what it means to "do it right." And those beliefs often show up in our parenting, especially during transitions and moments of resistance.

This chapter is an invitation to gently reflect:

- What did routine feel like to you as a child?
- What feels grounding now, and what feels constraining?
- When your child resists the flow of the day, what gets stirred up inside?

There's no one right way to structure your day. But there is a way to bring intention and awareness to it, so your child feels emotionally supported, and you feel more at ease. Routines don't need to be perfect. They don't even need to be rigid. But when they are predictable, flexible, and infused with emotional connection, they become more than just tasks to get through. They become touch-points of trust.

In the Slumberkins world, **Sloth** reminds us that daily routines can be soft, safe places to land—especially during the times when emotions run high. That's why this chapter helps you explore both the "how" and the "why" behind your family's rhythms. You'll be guided to reflect on your past, notice what your child is communicating through their behavior, and gently shape routines that foster both security and autonomy.

We'll also meet families who thrive on structure and those who prefer to flow. You'll explore your own "routine personality," and find strategies that help your family come into greater balance. Whether you're introducing routines for the first time or hoping to find more peace in the ones you already have, this chapter will meet you right where you are.

Because routines aren't just about what your child is doing. They're about what your child believes. Let's explore how to build those beliefs together.

"I am safe."

"I know what to expect."

"I can do this on my own."

WHY ROUTINES MATTER FOR CORE BELIEFS ....

Routines and structure are deeply tied to the **core beliefs of safety and autonomy**.

- **Safety:** Knowing what comes next helps children feel secure and confident in their world. Predictability supports a sense of **trust and stability**.
- **Autonomy:** Routines provide opportunities for kids to develop **independence**, gradually taking ownership of self-care and daily tasks.

Lack of structure in early childhood can shape core beliefs like:

☒ *"The world is unpredictable and unsafe."* → Leads to anxiety and insecurity.

☒ *"I have no control over my life."* → Can result in power struggles and resistance to authority.

Excessive structure, on the other hand, can lead to:

☒ *"I must follow strict rules or things will fall apart."* → Can foster perfectionism or fear of mistakes.

☒ *"I can't do things on my own."* → May limit a child's confidence in their capabilities.

Self-Reflection: Where Do You Fall on the Structure Spectrum?

Journaling prompts:

- Growing up, was my home highly structured, totally flexible, or somewhere in between?
- How did that impact how safe or independent I felt as a child?
- What aspects of my upbringing around routine do I want to continue? What do I want to change?
- When my child resists routine, what emotions come up for me? (Frustration? Anxiety? A sense of failure?)

Activity: A Day in Two Worlds

Instead of categorizing yourself, try walking through two short, imagined mornings—and just *notice* what comes up in your body and mind. Which one feels more like home to you?

Scene 1: The Structured Start

The alarm goes off at the same time it always does. The coffee's already brewing. Your child knows the steps—get dressed, brush teeth, eat breakfast—and follows the familiar flow. There's a checklist or a chart by the door, and everyone knows what's expected. You feel a sense of order. Predictability. A little control. But when something unexpected pops up—a shoe is missing, a meltdown begins—you notice your body tighten. The schedule matters, and disruptions feel stressful.

Scene 2: The Flowing Morning

You wake up naturally, or your child crawls into bed. The morning unfolds based on energy and needs. Maybe breakfast happens before getting dressed. Maybe there's music playing, or time to build with blocks before brushing teeth. There's less pressure to be on time, and more space to go with the moment. But when things feel chaotic or slow, you notice a sense of overwhelm. Uncertainty. You crave more structure, but resist rigidity.

Now take a breath and ask yourself:
- Which scene felt more comfortable? Which one brought tension?
- Where do you find yourself most days? Where do you *want* to be?
- What would it feel like to borrow a little from the other side?

This isn't about choosing one way to be. It's about noticing what you need—and what your child needs—to feel both safe and free.

Creating Balance: Strategies Based on Your Routine Style

If You Thrive on Routine (but Need More Flexibility)

Core Belief to Build: *"I can be flexible, and things will still be okay."*

Activities to introduce more spontaneity:

- **Surprise Switch Day:** Once a week, let your child pick an activity that replaces part of your usual routine.
- **Choose-Your-Own-Adventure Mornings:** Give your child two or three choices for how to start their day.
- **Yes Day (Within Limits!):** Say "yes" to small, fun requests that don't disrupt core routines.
- **Dinnertime Role Reversal:** Let your child help decide what's for dinner (within reasonable choices).

If You Struggle with Routine (but Need More Structure)
Core Belief to Build: *"Structure supports, it doesn't restrict."*

Activities to strengthen routine:
- **Visual Routine Chart:** Use pictures for younger kids, checklists for older ones.
- **Routine "Gamification":** Make tasks fun (racing to get shoes on, setting a timer for cleanup).
- **Anchor Points:** If full schedules overwhelm you, focus on just three predictable moments: morning, mealtime, and bedtime.
- **Theme Days:** Assign fun themes to weekdays (e.g., "Try Something New Tuesday").

Activities for All Ages

Each activity supports the core beliefs of **safety** and **autonomy** while making routines enjoyable and emotionally nourishing.

Babies (0–18 Months)

Why? Predictability builds safety and security. Babies learn what to expect through repeated, loving rituals, and those become their first tools for emotional regulation.

Activity 1: The Comfort Cue

Choose a consistent phrase, melody, or motion you repeat before naps or bedtime. Something as simple as "It's time to get cozy. You are safe and loved," said while rocking or laying them down, can become a powerful signal of rest. Over time, this repeated cue helps your baby associate those words with calm and comfort. It becomes a soothing bridge from your presence to sleep–and eventually, something they carry into their self-soothing toolbox as they grow.

Activity 2: Slow-Motion Snuggles

Very young brains organize around rhythmic sensory input. Extra-slow, repetitive movement, paired with gentle touch, lowers heart rate and teaches self-soothing.

- After the "Comfort Cue," cradle your baby and sway *exceptionally* slowly–about one gentle rock every five seconds.

- As you sway, trace a small circle between their shoulder blades with two fingers and whisper the Sloth mantra: *"Breathe in calm, breathe out ease. My body knows how to rest and release."*
- End by pausing completely for a full breath before laying them down.

Over time, the exaggerated slowness itself becomes a somatic signal that it's safe to relax, making future transitions (car seat, doctor visits, bedtime with another caregiver) smoother.

Toddlers (18 Months–3 Years)

Why? Establishing autonomy in small, manageable ways helps toddlers feel confident and capable while still needing the structure you provide.

Activity 1: Routine Helper

Offer your child simple choices during routine moments: "Would you like the blue pajamas or the dinosaur ones?" or "Do you want to brush your teeth before or after your bath?" Giving choice within boundaries builds confidence and helps toddlers feel like respected participants in their day, rather than passive passengers.

Activity 2: Routine Box

Create a special bin or basket with favorite "transition tools" for key parts of the day–like a bedtime book, a toothbrush song, or a cuddly toy they use to say goodbye in the morning. This not only makes routines more fun but also builds emotional predictability. The items become comforting anchors that help toddlers move from one activity to the next with more ease (and fewer power struggles).

Little Kids (3–5 Years)

Why? Knowing what's coming next gives kids a sense of control and safety, which can reduce resistance and increase cooperation during transitions.

Activity 1: Routine Race

Turn routine steps into mini games: "Let's see who can put their socks on the fastest!" or "Can you brush your teeth before I finish this song?" Adding playful energy helps release some of the stress from transitions and shifts your child's focus from "I don't want to" to "Let's do this together."

Activity 2: Routine Treasure Map

Draw a simple visual map of your child's routine (like: wake up → get dressed → eat breakfast → brush teeth). Let them place a sticker or color in a symbol each time they complete a step. This gives children a sense of mastery and momentum, turning the routine into something they can track and take pride in.

Big Kids (5–13 Years)

Why? Inviting kids into conversations about routines gives them ownership, strengthens executive function, and builds self-trust—skills they'll carry for life.

Activity 1: Routine Negotiation

Once a week, invite your child to propose a small change in their routine. For example: "Can I switch my reading time to after breakfast?" or "Can I set my own alarm tomorrow?" This shows them that their voice matters and helps build self-regulation within the safety of your guidance. You're giving them a say without letting go of the structure they still need.

Activity 2: Routine Role Reversal

Once a week, let your child be the "parent" during part of the routine—whether it's guiding bedtime steps or leading the morning rush. This encourages empathy, leadership, and even a little humor. It also gives you insight into what they've absorbed about routine and connection, from watching you.

AFFIRMATION TO REINFORCE CORE BELIEFS ||||||||||||||||||||||||||||||||||||||||||||||||||||||||||||||||||

*"When we have a routine,
I know what to do.
I am cared for and loved
by me and you."*

Personalized Routine Plan

- What's one **small change** I can make to bring more balance to my family's routines?
- How can I model flexibility *or* structure in a healthy way?

Key takeaways:

- Structure provides **security**; flexibility allows for **growth**.
- The goal is **not perfection, but balance**.

CHAPTER 3

Building Connections: The Power of Belonging

Refer to CHAPTER 7 **of** All Feelings Welcome *for deeper learning and under-standing about this concept.*

It's easy to move through the day in survival mode–packing lunches, answering a thousand questions, handling meltdowns, and squeezing in one more bedtime story when you're running on fumes. Parenting is full of doing. But underneath all of it, your child is quietly asking a question: "Am I safe here?" and "Do I matter to you?"

Whether it's in the chaos of the morning rush or a quiet moment at night, your relationship with your child is forming the blueprint for how they'll relate to others–and themselves. Their early experiences with connection (or disconnection) shape powerful beliefs like "I am lovable" or "I have to earn love."

In this chapter, we invite you to reflect on how connection shaped your own sense of belonging growing up–and how it's shaping your child's sense of belonging now. Did love feel stable and unconditional in your childhood? Was it something you earned or something you simply received? Often, we carry those early messages with us, even if we aren't aware of it. And in parenting, they can show up in surprising ways: how close we allow ourselves to get, how we respond when our child needs comfort, how much space we give ourselves to feel vulnerable.

One of the most important truths we share in *All Feelings Welcome* is that belonging is not a one-time achievement or something reserved for the "lucky" few. It is something we can grow into–and grow back into–again and again, at any age.

Our Slumberkins character **Otter** embodies this beautifully. Otter reminds us that love and attachment–not just biology–are what create families. Some children are born into families where connection feels safe and secure from the start. Others must find–or rebuild–that sense of family as they grow. What matters most is this: Every child deserves to know that they belong. That they are worthy of love. And that they can build a "heart family" made up of safe, caring people who see and value them fully.

By teaching children what connection feels like–through our everyday presence, care, and repair–we help lay the foundation for healthy relationships they will choose and build throughout their lives. It doesn't guarantee that they'll never face hurt or disconnection. But it does mean they'll have the tools to return to themselves and find their way back to belonging.

This chapter is about deepening that foundation. It's not about adding more to your to-do list–it's about noticing and nurturing what's already there. Because connection doesn't require perfection. It just needs presence, curiosity, and love.

Let's begin.

Children form core beliefs about relationships based on early experiences:

Positive connections create beliefs like:
> "I am lovable just as I am."
> "I belong."
> "People will show up for me."

Disconnection or inconsistent relationships can create beliefs like:
> "I have to earn love."
> "I am not important."
> "People always leave."

These beliefs affect how children navigate friendships, school, and eventually, their adult relationships.

Self-Reflection: Your Relationship with Connection

Journaling prompts:
- How did my family express love when I was growing up?
- Was I encouraged to talk about my feelings, or was I expected to "tough it out"?
- Did I feel safe and accepted in my relationships, or did I have to prove my worth?
- How do I react when my child seeks attention or comfort? Do I welcome it, feel annoyed, or feel unsure how to respond?

- What messages do I want to pass down about connection and love?

Connection Audit: Circle the relationships you find easiest.

- With my child
- With my partner
- With friends
- With my own parents

Where do I feel the most challenged? Why?

Reflection question:
When it comes to connection, what part of it feels the hardest for me–giving it, receiving it, or trusting it will last? Your answer can be a window into the beliefs you may have learned early on–beliefs that are still shaping your relationships today.

Creating Balance: Strengthening Connection Where You Need It Most

If You Struggle with Emotional Connection

Core Belief to Build: *"I am safe to connect and be vulnerable."*

Activities to strengthen emotional bonding:

- **The "One More" Rule:** When your child asks for a hug, an extra bedtime story, or five more minutes of play, say "yes" when you can.
- **Daily "You Matter" Moment:** Each day, take 60 seconds to tell your child one thing you love about them.
- **Check-in Jar:** Create a jar with feeling words (e.g., happy, sad, excited). Each person picks one and shares about their day.

If You Over-Function in Relationships (People-Pleasing or Fixing)

Core Belief to Build: *"I don't have to do everything to be loved."*

This version speaks directly to the heart of what's often driving over-functioning: the fear that love is earned through effort or self-sacrifice. It gently challenges that belief by affirming that *being* is enough—not just the doing.

Activities to create healthy boundaries:

- **Connection Without Fixing:** When your child is upset, practice just listening instead of jumping to solutions.

- **Independent Play Dates:** Encourage your child to have friend time without you leading the fun.
- **Model Self-Care:** Verbally name when you take a break for yourself. ("I'm going to read because I need some quiet time.")

Activities for All Ages

Each activity supports the core belief of belonging while fostering connection.

Babies (0–18 Months)

Why? Babies learn connection through physical closeness and responsiveness.

Activity 1: The Heartbeat Hold

Hold your baby against your chest so they can feel your heartbeat. This simple act reinforces safety and secure attachment. Hum your favorite song and rock them. These are all great ways to stimulate attachment for both you and baby.

Activity 2: Mirror Moments

Sit face-to-face with your baby and gently mimic their facial expressions and sounds. Smile when they smile. Coo when they coo. Repeat small gestures like sticking out your tongue or blinking slowly. This type of attuned mirroring builds emotional connection and helps your baby begin to recognize themselves as *seen, valued,* and *important* in your presence.

Toddlers (18 Months–3 Years)

Why? Toddlers need to feel connected while exploring independence.

Activity 1: Secret Handshake

Create a simple, playful handshake—maybe it's a high five, a fist bump, a pinky promise, or even a silly finger tap routine. Use it during transitions like drop-off, bedtime, or when saying goodbye. This small, consistent ritual becomes a tangible symbol of connection. It offers reassurance during separation and helps your toddler carry a piece of your relationship with them—even when you're not physically there.

Activity: Stuffed Animal Check-In

Use a favorite stuffed animal to explore emotions together. You might say, "Bear looks a little sad today. What do you think Bear needs?" Or "Bear had a really fun day–can you tell me why?" By externalizing feelings through the stuffed animal, toddlers can explore their inner world in a way that feels safe and playful. It also gives insights into how your child is processing experiences, especially if they aren't fully verbal yet.

Little Kids (3–5 Years)

Why? Playful rituals strengthen bonds and reinforce belonging.

Activity 1: The Love List

Sit down with your child and take turns naming things you love about each other–big or small. Write them down or draw pictures together, and hang your list somewhere you'll both see it every day. This simple activity helps your child *hear and see* their lovability reflected back to them. Over time, it builds a foundation of self-worth and lets them know they're cherished just for being themselves.

Activity 2: Switch Roles

Let your child "be the parent" for 10 minutes. Maybe they tuck *you* in, pack a pretend lunch for you, or remind you to brush your teeth. This playful role reversal boosts empathy and allows children to explore responsibility and care from a new perspective. It's also a chance for them to express what they've learned about connection–through the way they nurture you.

Little Kids (5–13 Years)

Why? At this stage, kids start questioning their worth and belonging.

Activity 1: Connection Calendar

Work together to create a "connection calendar." Let your child pick one time each week that's just for the two of you–no distractions, no multitasking. This dedicated space tells your child: *You matter to me. I choose you.* Even 20 minutes of focused time can leave a lasting impression and help them feel secure and prioritized.

Activity 2: Would You Rather—Feelings Edition

Create a set of playful, meaningful "Would You Rather" questions that explore values and emotional preferences.

Examples:

"Would you rather be brave or kind?"
"Would you rather have a big group of friends or one best friend?"
"Would you rather help someone or have someone help you?"

These questions invite your child into deeper conversations, without pressure. It gives them language to talk about who they are and what matters to them, while reinforcing their sense of self and belonging.

AFFIRMATION TO REINFORCE CORE BELIEFS ....

"I am safe, I am loved,
my connections are strong.
I have always been wanted,
I always belong."

Personalized Connection Plan

- What's one **small way** I can show up more intentionally in my child's world?
- How do I want my child to feel in our relationship?
- What connection rituals can we start today?

Key takeaway:

- Connection doesn't have to be grand—small, consistent moments create deep belonging.

CHAPTER 4

Mindfulness: Sitting with Feelings, Not Pushing Them Away

Refer to CHAPTER 8 of **All Feelings Welcome** *for deeper learning and understanding about this concept.*

There's a moment in every parent's day—maybe more than one—when things spiral just a little too fast. A toy thrown across the room, tears at drop-off, a refusal to put on shoes when you're already late. Your breath shortens. Your mind races. Your body tightens. And in that moment, the question becomes: "Can I pause here, or will I power through?"

In *All Feelings Welcome*, we explore mindfulness not as a practice for the "perfect" parent, but as a gift we can give ourselves and our children in the midst of real life. It's the ability to notice—without judgment—what's happening inside us, and then to choose presence over reaction. It's not about becoming calm all the time. It's about building a habit of *returning* to ourselves, over and over again, with compassion.

For many of us, this was never modeled. We were taught to keep going, tough it out, push past discomfort. But when we parent from that place, we miss the magic that lives in the moment between reaction and response. The space where we can say, "I see what's happening—and I can stay here with it."

Children learn emotional regulation by watching us regulate our own. When we slow down enough to name our feelings, breathe through tension, or simply say, "This is hard," we teach our kids that they can do the same. That feelings aren't problems—they're invitations to connect.

Our Slumberkins character **Yeti** reminds us that calming down doesn't mean shutting down. Yeti shows us how to create rituals of stillness, find peace in the middle of big emotions, and ground ourselves with gentleness rather than control.

This chapter is your invitation to explore mindfulness, not as another thing to get right, but as a way to bring more ease into the hardest parts of your day. You don't need quiet to practice mindfulness. You just need curiosity, a breath, and the willingness to come back to yourself—even in the middle of the grocery aisle.

Let's begin.

Mindfulness–being present and aware without judgment–helps shape core beliefs about emotions and self-control.

Children who experience mindful parenting learn:

> "All my emotions are okay."
> "I can calm my body and mind."
> "I am safe, even when I feel big feelings."

Without emotional regulation support, children may internalize beliefs like:

> "Big feelings are bad."
> "I have to suppress emotions to be accepted."
> "I can't control my reactions."

Mindfulness helps both parent and child build the skills to pause, reflect, and regulate emotions instead of reacting impulsively.

Self-Reflection: Your Relationship with Emotional Regulation

Journaling prompts:

- How were emotions handled in my childhood?
- Was I taught to sit with emotions, or was I expected to "move on" quickly?
- When my child has big emotions, what is my instinctual response? (To fix? To ignore? To get overwhelmed?)
- How do I personally respond to stress? Do I have calming strategies, or do I push through?

Mindfulness self-check:

- I feel most present when:

  _____

- I feel the most reactive when:

  _____

- One way I could pause before reacting is:

  _____

Reflection question:

When emotions run high, what part feels hardest for me—staying calm, feeling my own feelings, or knowing what to say? Your answer can offer insight into the emotional patterns you learned growing up—and how those patterns might show up in parenting today.

Creating Balance: Strategies Based on Your Mindfulness Style

If You Tend to Over-Control Emotions (Avoidance or Perfectionism)

Core Belief to Build: *"I can sit with emotions without needing to fix or suppress them."*

Activities to build emotional awareness:

- **Pause Before the Fix Challenge:** When your child expresses a big feeling, resist the urge to immediately problem-solve. Try saying, "That sounds really hard. I'm here with you."
- **Feelings Mapping:** Throughout the day, name your emotions out loud: "I'm feeling a little overwhelmed right now." This helps normalize emotional awareness for both of you.
- **Mindful Transitions:** Before switching from one activity to another (work to home, morning to school), take 30 seconds to pause and breathe. This helps you re-enter the moment with intention.

If You Struggle with Emotional Regulation (Reacting Quickly or Feeling Overwhelmed)

Core Belief to Build: *"I can slow down and respond with intention."*

Activities to practice self-regulation:

- **Three-Deep-Breath Rule:** In moments of tension, pause and take three deep breaths before responding. This short pause can prevent reaction and create space for choice.
- **Sensory Grounding:** When you're overwhelmed, pause and name these: one thing you see, hear, feel, and smell. This technique helps anchor your nervous system in the present.
- **Five-Minute Meditation Breaks:** Set aside just five minutes to listen to a calming meditation or to sit in silence. Even short pauses can restore clarity and regulate stress.

Activities for All Ages

Each activity supports self-awareness and emotional regulation.

Babies (0–18 Months)

Why? Infants co-regulate with caregivers, learning calmness through presence.

Activity 1: Breath Sync

Hold your baby close—skin-to-skin if possible—and take slow, steady breaths. Your baby will naturally begin to match your rhythm, helping them regulate through your nervous system. This kind of calming presence is the earliest form of mindfulness: It helps your baby feel safe in their body.

Activity 2: Sunrise and Sunset

During morning and bedtime routines, pause together by a window. Look out quietly for a moment and name what you see. This small daily ritual helps both of you slow down and adds stillness to your shared rhythm.

Toddlers (18 Months–3 Years)

Why? Teaching body awareness builds early emotional regulation skills.

Activity 1: Teddy Belly Breathing

Have your toddler lie on their back and place a stuffed animal on their belly. Say, "Let's help Teddy ride the waves!" and guide them to breathe in and out slowly. This playful practice helps toddlers begin to connect their breath to a feeling of calm.

Activity 2: Animal Walks

Channel big energy through movement: stomp like an elephant, stretch like a cat, hop like a bunny. This lets your toddler explore emotional energy through play—and begin learning how movement can regulate big feelings.

Little Kids (3–5 Years)

Why? Naming emotions and using the body to regulate supports self-awareness.

Activity 1: Feelings Freeze Dance

Play music and call out an emotion, like happy, grumpy, or excited. Your child dances how that emotion feels, then freezes like a statue. This playful activity helps normalize all kinds of feelings and teaches that emotions can be moved through, not suppressed.

Activity 2: Calm Down Jars

Make a sensory bottle together using water, glitter, and a bit of glue. Shake it up and watch it settle. The swirling glitter becomes a visual metaphor for emotional intensity—eventually settling, just like feelings do.

Big Kids (5–13 Years)

Why? This age group benefits from mindfulness tools that promote focus, self-awareness, and emotional expression.

Activity 1: Mindful Moments Challenge

Each day, choose one ordinary moment—brushing teeth, eating lunch, walking outside—and practice noticing your surroundings. "What do you see? Hear? Feel?" This builds the skill of presence and helps kids realize mindfulness can happen anytime, anywhere.

Activity 2: The Thought Journal

Invite your child to write down one moment from the day that felt overwhelming, and how they responded. Then write one thing that helped. This practice supports reflection, helps children process emotions, and builds confidence in their ability to manage hard moments.

AFFIRMATION TO REINFORCE CORE BELIEFS ....

"With my heart open
and my mind open too,
I explore the world,
I am present with you."

Personalized Mindfulness Plan

- What's one way I can model mindfulness in my daily life?
- How can I support my child in slowing down and regulating emotions?

Key takeaway:

- Mindfulness is not about removing emotions—it's about learning to sit with them, safely and compassionately.

CHAPTER 5

Emotional Courage: Embracing All Feelings

Refer to CHAPTER 9 of **All Feelings Welcome** *for deeper learning and understanding about this concept.*

Emotions don't always arrive in gentle waves. Sometimes they crash—loud, messy, and full of confusion. Maybe your child is sobbing after a hard day, yelling in frustration, or withdrawing into silence with feelings they can't name. These moments call for something powerful, not perfection, but presence. *Emotional courage.*

Emotional courage is the ability to sit with feelings, even the uncomfortable ones. It's the capacity to be angry, sad, scared, or uncertain—and still feel safe, still feel loved. But this kind of courage doesn't grow in a vacuum. It's built in the small, everyday moments when we respond with empathy instead of panic, when we say, "It's okay to feel this way. I'm right here."

For many of us, this wasn't how we were raised. Maybe we learned to suppress our feelings to stay out of trouble. Maybe we were praised for being the *easy* child. Maybe no one ever taught us that emotions were safe to feel. So when our children show us their biggest feelings, we may find ourselves repeating old patterns—rushing to distract, fix, or quiet what feels too loud inside us.

But emotional courage can be learned. It can be modeled. And it can be passed down—by breaking the silence, by normalizing vulnerability, and by staying soft in moments we were once taught to harden.

In *All Feelings Welcome*, we talk about how core beliefs around feelings are shaped early, and how caregivers can be the safest place for kids to fall apart. When we hold space without rushing to solutions, we show our children that emotions are not problems. They're signals. And they're worth listening to.

Our Slumberkins character **Ibex** represents this inner strength. Ibex doesn't push feelings aside—he faces them with honesty, compassion, and quiet bravery. He reminds kids that courage isn't the absence of fear—it's feeling the fear and staying present anyway.

This chapter will help you reflect on your emotional blueprint and build a home where emotional bravery is not only welcomed but celebrated. Not by doing it perfectly, but by showing up again and again with love, truth, and the willingness to feel.

Let's begin.

Emotional courage is the ability to embrace and express emotions fully, even when it's uncomfortable. It builds resilience and helps children understand that all emotions are valid and have a purpose.

Children who develop emotional courage learn:

"I can handle all my emotions."

"Vulnerability is strength."

"I don't have to hide my feelings to be loved."

Without emotional courage, children may internalize beliefs like:

"Big emotions are bad."

"I should be tough and not show feelings."

"If I express sadness or fear, I am weak."

Self-Reflection: Your Relationship with Emotional Courage

Journaling prompts:

- What emotions did I feel safe expressing as a child?
- Were there feelings I was told to "get over" or "push down"?
- When I see my child struggling with emotions, what is my instinct? (To fix? To distract? To ignore?)
- Do I associate vulnerability with strength or weakness? Why?

Emotional Courage Audit: Check the emotions you express most easily.

- Happiness ☺
- Anger ☹
- Sadness ☹
- Fear ☹

Which emotions feel hardest for you to show? Why?

Reflection question:

When was the last time I showed a vulnerable emotion in front of my child? What did I learn from that moment?

Creating Balance: Strategies Based on Your Emotional Patterns

If You Tend to Suppress Emotions

Core Belief to Build: *"All feelings are safe to feel and express."*

Activities to build emotional awareness:

- **Daily Feelings Check-in:** At the end of each day, name one emotion you felt and share it aloud. This simple practice models the concept that emotions are natural and worth acknowledging.
- **Pause Instead of Pushing Through:** When your child is upset, instead of saying, "You're fine," try "That sounds really tough. I hear you."
- **The "I Feel" Game:** At dinner or during quiet time, each person shares a moment when they felt happy, sad, and frustrated that day. This builds language and comfort around emotional expression.

If You Struggle with Overwhelming Emotions

Core Belief to Build: *"I can experience big emotions without being consumed by them."*

Activities to practice emotional regulation:

- **The 90-Second Rule:** Neuroscience tells us that intense emotions often pass within 90 seconds if we don't fuel them with thoughts. When overwhelmed, pause and breathe for 90 seconds before responding.
- **Body Awareness Check:** Notice where emotions show up physically–tight chest, clenched jaw, heavy shoulders. Teach your child to do the same by asking, "Where do you feel that in your body?"
- **Naming the Storm:** Help yourself and your child by saying, "I am feeling [emotion], but I am not my feelings." This reminds everyone that feelings are passing, not permanent.

Activities for All Ages

Each activity helps children welcome emotions, process them, and build resilience.

Babies (0-18 Months)

Why? Babies learn that emotions are safe when caregivers respond with calm presence.

Activity 1: Mirroring Emotions

When your baby smiles, frowns, or looks startled, mirror their expression and gently name what you see: "You look surprised!" or "That was loud, huh?"

This helps babies begin connecting facial expressions to emotions, which is the foundation for emotional recognition.

Activity 2: The Calm Voice

When your baby cries, use a slow, steady voice: "I hear you. I'm right here." Even if they can't understand the words, your tone communicates safety and acceptance. Over time, this model suggests that emotions are not something to fear or stop—they're safe to express.

Toddlers (18 Months-3 Years)

Why? Toddlers need help labeling and moving through emotions.

Activity 1: Feelings Faces

Draw or print simple faces showing different emotions—happy, sad, mad, scared. Ask, "Which face looks like how you feel right now?" This gives toddlers a tool to name their inner experience, helping them feel seen and supported.

Activity 2: Stuffed Animal Feelings

Use a favorite toy to explore emotions. "Bear is sad today. What do you think Bear needs?" Toddlers often express more through imaginative play than direct answers. This encourages empathy and gives your child practice responding to emotions in a nurturing way.

Little Kids (3-5 Years)

Why? Young children benefit from physical movement to process emotions.

Activity 1: Dragon Breath

Say, "Pretend you're a dragon. Take a big breath in . . . now blow out your fire!" This helps introduce deep breathing in a fun, embodied way. Over time, you can use "dragon breath" to help with calming down during big feelings.

Activity 2: Act Out Feelings

Take turns acting out different emotions and guessing what they are—happy, worried, tired, excited. Use voices, faces, and even body posture. This normalizes a wide range of feelings and builds emotional fluency through movement and imagination.

Big Kids (5–13 Years)

Why? Older children need tools to express emotions in a healthy way.

Activity 1: Bravery Journal

Encourage your child to write (or draw) about a time they felt something deeply—like sadness, fear, or anger—and moved through it. This helps build self-awareness, normalizes emotional processing, and reinforces the idea that strength and vulnerability can coexist.

Activity 2: The Hard Conversation Game

Role-play tricky emotional scenarios together, such as asking a friend for space, telling a parent they feel overwhelmed, or standing up for themselves. This gives kids a safe way to practice emotional courage and develop language for hard but important conversations.

AFFIRMATION TO REINFORCE CORE BELIEFS ....

*"I feel deeply.
I am brave and I am strong.
When I welcome my feelings,
I can never go wrong."*

Personalized Emotional Courage Plan

- What's one way I can model emotional courage for my child?
- How do I want my child to feel about their emotions?

Key takeaway:

- Bravery isn't about avoiding feelings—it's about feeling them fully, and knowing you're still safe and loved.

CHAPTER 6

Gratitude: Cultivating a Mindset of Abundance

Refer to CHAPTER 10 *of* All Feelings Welcome *for deeper learning and under-standing about this concept.*

Gratitude isn't just about saying thank you. It's about what we notice—what we choose to pay attention to. It's about whether we move through life grasping for what's missing, or pause long enough to feel the goodness of what's already here: sunlight on your face, a laugh shared at the dinner table, the small act of kindness from a stranger when your arms were too full.

In *All Feelings Welcome*, we talk about gratitude not as a polite behavior, but as a perspective. A practice. A way of seeing the world through the lens of *enoughness*—not because everything is perfect, but because presence is more powerful than perfection.

Many of us were raised with messages that made gratitude feel like a rule: *Be grateful for what you have. Don't ask for more. Someone else has it worse.* And while these messages were often well-intentioned, they may have taught us that we should silence our needs instead of exploring them. Or that gratitude meant not wanting, not hoping, not reaching.

But true gratitude is expansive. It doesn't shrink us. It reminds us of what's possible—even in difficult moments. It softens the edges of disappointment. It allows joy to sit beside grief, and enoughness to coexist with desire.

Gratitude helps children develop essential core beliefs: "The world is full of good things." "I don't need more to be happy." "I can feel satisfied with what I have." And when practiced with consistency, it builds emotional resilience and guards against comparison, entitlement, and the feeling that love or joy must be earned.

Our Slumberkins character **Honey Bear** embodies this energy beautifully. Honey Bear helps children focus on connection, not consumption. Through gentle rituals and shared appreciation, she reminds families that gratitude is not about having more—it's about seeing more.

This chapter will help you to reflect on your own story with gratitude and to begin crafting rituals of appreciation in your home. Because gratitude is not just a feeling—it's a way of being. And it's one of the greatest gifts we can give our children, and ourselves.

Let's begin.

Gratitude is more than just saying "thank you"—it's a mindset that shifts focus from what we lack to what we have.

Children who practice gratitude develop beliefs like:

"I have enough."

"I am surrounded by kindness."

"The world is full of good things."

Without gratitude, children may develop beliefs like:

"I need more to be happy."

"I deserve what I have, I don't need to appreciate it."

"People owe me things."

Self-Reflection: Your Relationship with Gratitude

Journaling prompts:

- How was gratitude practiced in my family growing up?
- Did I feel like I had enough, or was there a sense of "never enough" (money, time, love, attention)?
- Do I often focus on what I'm missing, or do I take time to appreciate what I have?
- When my child asks for more (toys, treats, attention), what emotions come up for me?

Gratitude awareness check:

- I feel most grateful when:

_____

- I struggle with gratitude when:

_____

- One way I could model gratitude more intentionally is:

_____

Reflection question:

What story do I tell myself when I don't have what I want? What does that say about my relationship with abundance?

Creating Balance: Strategies Based on Your Gratitude Patterns

If You Struggle with a Scarcity Mindset
Core Belief to Build: *"I have enough, and I am enough."*

Activities to cultivate abundance:

- **Gratitude Reframe:** When you catch yourself thinking, "I wish we had more," try shifting to "I'm grateful we have." This gentle reframing builds awareness of what's already present.
- **Daily Gratitude Moment:** Choose one small moment at the end of the day to say aloud: "Something I appreciated today was. . ."
- **Noticing the Gifts Around You:** Go on a gratitude walk and name five things in nature you're thankful for–sunlight, shadows, birdsong, a flower. This reconnects you to the world's everyday beauty.

If You Over-Emphasize Material Gratitude (Teaching Kids to "Just Be Thankful")
Core Belief to Build: *"Gratitude is about connection, not just possessions."*

Activities to deepen gratitude:

- **Kindness Chain:** Every time someone does something thoughtful, add a link to a paper gratitude chain. Watch it grow as kindness ripples through your home.

- **Appreciation Notes:** Leave handwritten notes of thanks around the house—on lunchboxes, mirrors, or pillows. Model thoughtful acknowledgment.
- **Experience Over Things:** Instead of rewarding with a new toy, plan a shared experience. A gratitude walk, baking together, or a kindness scavenger hunt can leave a deeper imprint.

Activities for All Ages

Each activity supports gratitude as a mindset, not just a reaction.

Babies (0–18 Months)

Why? Babies learn gratitude through emotional warmth and connection.

Activity 1: Thankful Touch

While feeding, rocking, or cuddling, gently speak out loud what you're appreciating in the moment: "I love how cozy we are right now." This pairs sensory connection with verbal affection, helping your baby associate calm and gratitude with the relationship.

Activity 2: Morning Gratitude Greeting

Every morning, say something simple and warm like, "Good morning! I'm so grateful for you." These consistent messages help create an early sense of being loved, cherished, and appreciated.

Toddlers (18 Months–3 Years)

Why? Toddlers are just beginning to mimic gratitude language and recognize patterns.

Activity 1: Gratitude Handprint

Paint your toddler's hand and press it onto paper. Ask, "What makes you happy today?" and write their response inside the handprint. This helps them start linking feelings of joy to experiences, people, or objects—not just to getting "more."

Activity 2: Thank You, Teddy

Model gratitude in imaginative play by thanking a stuffed animal: "Thank you, Bear, for your cuddles today!" This encourages toddlers to express appreciation in their own ways, especially through play.

Little Kids (3–5 Years)

Why? This age group begins connecting gratitude with relationships, not just objects.

Activity 1: The Love List

Sit with your child and make a list of things they love about each family member. Add drawings or photos, and read it together. This helps them understand that people are what we value most–not just what people give us.

Activity 2: Noticing the Helpers

Each day, talk about someone who helped them, like a teacher, a friend, or a neighbor. Ask, "How did that feel?" This builds awareness of everyday kindness and encourages gratitude for people, not just for possessions.

Big Kids (5–13 Years)

Why? Older children can reflect more deeply on emotional experiences and lasting gratitude.

Activity 1: Gratitude Journal

Invite your child to write down one thing they're grateful for each day–and *why* it matters to them. This builds a daily habit of noticing and appreciating even small things.

Activity 2: Gratitude Letter

Have your child write a letter to someone who has made a difference in their life–a coach, a teacher, a grandparent. Writing the letter (even if it's not sent) reinforces the power of expressing appreciation from the heart.

"I have all I need,
there are gifts all around.
I am grateful in my heart,
for the love I have found."

Personalized Gratitude Plan

- How can I integrate gratitude into my daily routine?
- What's one new gratitude habit I'd like to try with my child?

Key takeaway:

- Gratitude is a practice, not just a feeling–and it's something we can return to again and again, no matter the day.

CHAPTER 7

Self-Esteem: Embracing Worthiness

Refer to CHAPTER 11 of **All Feelings Welcome** *for deeper learning and understanding about this concept.*

Self-esteem isn't just about confidence or compliments. It's the quiet, steady belief that you are worthy of love–just as you are. It's knowing that you matter even when you mess up, fall short, or feel unsure of yourself. And for our children, self-esteem doesn't start with praise. It starts with presence. They will feel safe to be exactly who they are when they're with us.

In *All Feelings Welcome*, we explore how self-worth is built–not through achievements, but through connection. A child's sense of worth grows when they are seen, accepted, and held during both their joy and their struggle. When they learn that love doesn't disappear when they get it "wrong."

For many of us, self-esteem was shaped early–by how we were praised, corrected, or comforted. Maybe we felt celebrated when we succeeded, but unseen when we failed. Maybe we learned that being the "best" was the safest way to be loved. And without realizing it, those old stories can still guide our reactions today.

So when our child says, "I'm not good at this," or shrinks away from trying, we might rush in to fix, to cheerlead, or to push. But what they often need is something quieter: someone to sit with them and say, "I see you. I love you. You're enough, right here."

Our Slumberkins character **Bigfoot** was created to remind children–and caregivers–that they are always lovable, especially when they're feeling low. Bigfoot doesn't have all the answers, but he knows that what matters most is showing up with love that doesn't waver.

This chapter invites you to gently reflect on the roots of your own self-worth, and to explore new ways of nurturing your child's confidence through presence, empathy, and small moments of affirmation. Not for what they *do*–but simply for who they *are*.

Let's begin.

Self-esteem is the belief in one's own value and worthiness. Children develop self-esteem when they feel loved, valued, and capable–even in the face of mistakes or challenges.

Children with healthy self-esteem develop beliefs like:

> *"I am loved and lovable."*
>
> *"I am capable of trying new things."*
>
> *"I am enough, even when I make mistakes."*

Without a strong foundation of self-worth, children may internalize beliefs like:

> *"I have to prove my worth."*
>
> *"I am only valuable if I succeed."*
>
> *"I am not good enough."*

These beliefs influence everything, from friendships and learning to how they handle setbacks and failure.

Self-Reflection: Your Relationship with Self-Esteem

Journaling prompts:

- How was self-worth communicated in my family? Was love unconditional, or tied to achievements or behavior?
- Do I feel worthy as I am, or do I often seek validation from others?
- When my child struggles with self-doubt, what is my instinct? (To reassure? To push them harder? To avoid the conversation?)
- How do I respond to my own mistakes? With kindness or criticism?

Self-worth awareness check:

- I feel most confident when:

  _____

- I struggle with self-worth when:

  _____

- One way I could model self-esteem for my child is:

  _____

Reflection question:

When I make a mistake or fall short, what do I tell myself? What would I want my child to hear instead?

Creating Balance: Strategies Based on Your Self-Esteem Patterns

If You Struggled with Self-Worth as a Child
Core Belief to Build: *"I am enough, just as I am."*

Activities to reframe self-worth:
- **Positive Mirror Talk:** Each day, look in the mirror and say something kind about yourself—just as you are.
- **Rewriting Self-Talk:** When you hear the voice that says, "I should have done better," gently shift to "I did my best today. That's enough."
- **Modeling Growth Mindset:** When you make a mistake, say out loud, "That didn't go how I wanted, but I'm learning. I'll keep trying."

If You Tend to Tie Worth to Achievements (Perfectionism)
Core Belief to Build: *"I am valuable for who I am, not what I do."*

Activities to loosen achievement-based self-worth:
- **"Good Enough" Practice:** Intentionally do something imperfect—messy art, silly dancing, a relaxed dinner—and enjoy it without correcting.
- **Celebrate Effort, Not Outcome:** Praise your child for trying, practicing, or showing kindness, not just for getting it "right."
- **"What Went Well" Reflection:** At the end of the day, name three things that went well. Let them be small. Let them be enough.

Activities for All Ages

Each activity builds confidence, self-worth, and resilience.

Babies (0–18 Months)

Why? Infants learn self-worth through secure attachment and loving responsiveness.

Activity 1: The Love Whisper

As you hold, rock, or feed your baby, softly say affirming words: "You are so loved. You are wonderful just as you are." Even before they understand the words, your tone and consistency build a foundation of worth and emotional safety.

Activity 2: Responsive Play

Follow your baby's lead in play—imitate their coos, mirror their facial expressions, and engage at their pace. This lets your baby know: *You matter. I see you. I'm here.*

Toddlers (18 Months–3 Years)

Why? Toddlers develop confidence through independence and positive reinforcement.

Activity 1: I Can Do It!

Invite your toddler to try a simple task (putting on shoes, pouring water). Celebrate effort more than success: "You worked so hard on that!" This helps them connect persistence to pride—not just performance.

Activity 2: Stuffed Animal Encouragement

Use play to explore self-worth. Say, "Bear feels unsure. What can we say to help Bear feel better?" This gives toddlers language for compassion—and reinforces that needing encouragement is normal.

Little Kids (3–5 Years)

Why? This is a crucial stage for forming beliefs about worth and capability.

Activity 1: My Special Poster

Let your child create a poster about themselves—things they're good at, what they like, drawings of their favorite moments. Display it proudly. It becomes a mirror of self-acceptance and celebration.

Activity 2: Power Pose Practice

Teach your child a "superhero pose" for when they feel nervous—feet wide, hands on hips, head high. Practice together. This body-based strategy helps shift posture and mindset, offering a confidence boost from the inside out.

Big Kids (5–13 Years)

Why? Older kids begin comparing themselves to others and benefit from tools that center inner worth.

Activity 1: Success Journal

Encourage your child to write down one thing they did well each day, big or small. This reinforces effort and self-acknowledgment, especially when outside validation is missing.

Activity 2: Affirmation Jar

Write positive affirmations on slips of paper and keep them in a jar. Each morning, pull one together to start the day with confidence. This creates a daily habit of internalizing worth—and reminds them that encouragement is always available.

AFFIRMATION TO REINFORCE CORE BELIEFS

BIGFOOT

SELF-ESTEEM

"I am so loved.
This will always be true.
As I grow and I learn,
I love myself too."

Personalized Self-Esteem Plan

- How do I want my child to feel about themselves?
- What is one way I can model self-worth in my daily life?

Key takeaway:

- Self-esteem isn't about perfection—it's about knowing you are worthy, no matter what.

CHAPTER 8

Authenticity: Embracing Who You Are

Refer to CHAPTER 12 of **All Feelings Welcome** *for deeper learning and understanding about this concept.*

There's a quiet kind of magic in watching a child discover who they are. You see it in their bold outfit choices, their wild dance moves, the way they talk to bugs or ask questions that stop you in your tracks. These moments aren't just cute quirks. They're glimpses of something deeper: your child's authentic self beginning to shine.

And yet, somewhere along the way, so many of us learn to hide those parts of ourselves. We tone things down to avoid standing out. We say what's expected instead of what we really think. We look for belonging in all the places that ask us to shrink just a little bit to fit in.

In *All Feelings Welcome*, we talk about how authenticity is more than just "being yourself." It's about having the courage to stay connected to who you are, even when it's hard. It's the voice inside that says, "I know myself. I trust myself. I can be fully me and still be safe, loved, and accepted."

For some of us, this idea of safety in self-expression wasn't modeled growing up. Maybe you were the "easy one" who learned not to rock the boat. Maybe you stood out in a way that was misunderstood—or even rejected. And now, as a parent, you might find yourself unsure how to respond when your child expresses themselves in bold, unexpected, or nontraditional ways. It's okay. That uncertainty is part of the work.

Our Slumberkins character **Unicorn** reminds us that true strength comes from standing in our uniqueness. Unicorn doesn't just sparkle because she's magical—she sparkles because she's real. She doesn't hide the parts of herself that others might not understand. And when she's surrounded by friends who accept her fully, she shines even brighter.

This chapter is about making space for that kind of sparkle—not just for your child, but for you, too. It's about creating an environment where self-expression is celebrated, not corrected. Where curiosity replaces judgment. Where your child knows, in every fiber of their being, I'm safe to be exactly who I am.

Let's begin.

Why Authenticity Matters for Core Beliefs

WHY SELF-ESTEEM MATTERS FOR CORE BELIEFS ....

Authenticity means being true to yourself, even when it feels difficult or risky. It requires courage, self-trust, and a sense of belonging.

Children who develop authenticity build beliefs like:

> *"I am enough just as I am."*
> *"I don't need to change to be accepted."*
> *"Being different makes me special."*

Without authenticity, children may internalize beliefs like:

> *"I have to fit in to be loved."*
> *"If I show my true self, people will reject me."*
> *"It's safer to hide who I really am."*

When children feel safe to express themselves, they develop deeper friendships, resist peer pressure, and trust their inner voice.

Self-Reflection: Your Relationship with Authenticity

Journaling prompts:

- Was I encouraged to be myself as a child, or was I expected to fit in?
- Have I ever changed parts of myself to be accepted?
- Do I feel comfortable expressing my true opinions and emotions?
- How do I react when my child expresses themselves in a way that challenges societal norms or my expectations?

Authenticity awareness check:

- I feel most like myself when:

  _____

- I struggle to be authentic when:

  _____

- One way I can model authenticity for my child is:

  _____

Reflection question:

When have I held back or changed myself to feel accepted, how might that shape what I teach my child about being true to themselves?

Self-Reflection: Strategies Based on Your Authenticity Patterns

If You Struggled to Be Authentic as a Child
Core Belief to Build: *"I am safe to be myself."*

Activities to embrace authenticity:

- **Rewriting Old Stories:** Reflect on a time when you hid part of yourself to fit in. What would you say to that younger version of you now?
- **Authenticity Challenge:** Choose one way to express your true self this week–through your clothes, creativity, or voice. Let your child see you owning it.
- **Affirmation Practice:** Start your day with: "I am enough, just as I am." Invite your child to create their own version.

If You Tend to Encourage Conformity (Out of Concern for Your Child Fitting In)
Core Belief to Build: *"I can support my child's uniqueness while keeping them safe."*

Activities to celebrate differences:

- **Spot the Uniqueness:** Read books or watch short videos about real people who made an impact by being themselves–musicians, artists, activists, or inventors.
- **Family Identity Talk:** Have a conversation about what makes your family unique–your values, your quirks, your favorite traditions.

- **Encourage Self-Expression:** Offer freedom in areas like clothing, creative projects, or hairstyles—even if their choices surprise you. Let your support be louder than your worry.

Activities for All Ages

Each activity helps children trust their inner voice and feel safe expressing themselves.

Babies (0–18 Months)

Why? Babies begin forming their sense of identity through caregiver interactions.

Activity 1: Mirroring Joy

Notice what delights your baby—bubbles, a favorite toy, a sound—and mirror that joy with your face and voice. This tells them, "What lights you up matters. I see you."

Activity 2: Sing Their Name

Make up a simple, loving song using your baby's name and a positive trait (e.g., "Nora is joyful, Nora is strong!"). This early repetition helps connect identity with warmth, love, and acceptance.

Toddlers (18 Months–3 Years)

Why? Toddlers start asserting independence and forming preferences.

Activity 1: Pick and Play

Let your child choose between two toys, snacks, or books. Celebrate their choice out loud: "You picked the red one! That's a great decision." This builds decision-making skills and confidence in their inner voice.

Activity 2: Silly Style

Encourage them to dress up in bold, creative, or mismatched outfits—then wear something fun yourself. Celebrate how awesome and different everyone looks. This gives toddlers the message that self-expression is safe, fun, and valued.

Little Kids (3–5 Years)

Why? This age group begins comparing themselves to others and may adjust their behavior to fit in.

Activity 1: Tell Your Story

Ask your child to draw or narrate a story about a character who stays true to themselves, even when others try to change them. Then say, "That character is brave, just like you when you do what feels right."

Activity 2: Talent Show

Create a low-pressure talent show at home. Let your child share a song, dance, or silly trick—and be their biggest cheerleader. This reinforces that they're celebrated for who they are, not just what they can do.

Big Kids (5–13 Years)

Why? Older kids feel stronger peer pressure and need practice trusting themselves.

Activity 1: My Authentic Self List

Ask your child to write down:

- Three things they love about themselves
- Three things that make them different

   Talk about how those traits help them connect with others in real, lasting ways.

Activity 2: Role-Playing Peer Pressure

Practice simple scripts for tricky moments—like saying no, disagreeing respectfully, or staying true to themselves.

Example:
   "No thanks, I don't like that game," or *"I'm going to be myself, even if others don't get it."*

   These rehearsals build real-world courage and help make authenticity a practiced habit.

"I have my own magic,
my own inner light.
When I am true to myself,
it shines strong and bright."

Personalized Authenticity Plan

- What's one way I can encourage my child's self-expression?
- How can I model authenticity in my own life?

Key takeaway:

- Being authentic is an act of bravery. When we embrace who we are, we inspire others to do the same.

CHAPTER 9

Growth Mindset: Learning Through Challenges

Refer to CHAPTER 13 of **All Feelings Welcome** *for deeper learning and under-standing about this concept.*

There's something quietly powerful about watching a child try again. Whether they're reaching for a toy just out of grasp, trying to draw a star, or learning to tie their shoes–it's in these tiny acts of effort that something big is forming: belief. Belief that they can keep going, even when it's hard. Belief that mistakes are part of learning. Belief that struggling doesn't mean stopping.

But for many of us, those beliefs didn't come naturally. We may have grown up in environments where mistakes were something to be ashamed of. Where praise came only when we got it "right." Where it felt easier to give up than risk failing in front of someone else. Maybe we still carry those messages today.

In *All Feelings Welcome*, we share how emotional safety plays a key role in developing resilience. Children need to know they can try, fail, and try again–without losing connection or love. When we focus too much on outcomes–grades, goals, or "getting it right"–we unintentionally send the message that their value comes from achievement. But when we praise effort, celebrate progress, and normalize mistakes, we help them form a more powerful story: *I'm still learning–and that's enough.*

Our Slumberkins character **Narwhal** is all about embracing challenges. Narwhal doesn't give up when something's hard. He keeps trying–not because he's the best, but because he believes in his ability to grow. And when kids see that modeled through our words, actions, and encouragement, they begin to believe it too.

This chapter is about building that belief in your child–and maybe even in yourself. Because a growth mindset isn't about doing things perfectly. It's about trusting that each step forward (even the messy ones) is part of becoming.

Let's begin.

A growth mindset is the belief that abilities and intelligence can grow with effort, persistence, and learning from mistakes.

Children with a growth mindset develop beliefs like:

"Mistakes help me learn."

"I can get better with practice."

"Challenges make me stronger."

Without a growth mindset, children may internalize beliefs like:

"I'm either good at something or I'm not."

"If I fail, it means I'm not smart."

"Struggling means I should give up."

By teaching perseverance and grit—the ability to keep going even when things feel hard—we help children build resilience that will serve them for life.

Self-Reflection: Your Relationship with Learning and Perseverance

Journaling prompts:

- When I was a child, how did I react to challenges or failures?
- Was I praised more for effort or for getting things right?
- Do I avoid things I don't think I'll be good at?
- How do I respond when my child struggles with something new?

Growth mindset awareness check:

- I feel most confident when I:

  _____

- I feel frustrated when I:

  _____

- One way I could model perseverance is:

  _____

Reflection question:

When I struggle with something new, what story do I tell myself—and how might that influence the way I respond to my child's struggles?

Creating Balance: Strategies Based on Your Mindset Patterns

If You Tend to Avoid Challenges (Fear of Failure)
Core Belief to Build: *"Struggle is how I grow."*

Activities to reframe challenges:
- **Reframing Setbacks:** When you or your child says, "I can't do this," add the word "yet." It plants the seed of possibility.
- **The Learning Log:** Reflect on a time when you failed and what you learned. Share it with your child. It helps normalize failure as a teacher.
- **Try Something Hard (Together):** Choose a new skill–drawing, dancing, speaking a new language–and embrace being a beginner together.

If You Tie Success to Being Naturally Talented
Core Belief to Build: *"Hard work matters more than talent."*

Activities to reinforce effort over talent:
- **Effort-Focused Praise:** Shift from "You're so smart!" to "I love how hard you worked on that."
- **The Grit Challenge:** Choose a small, tough goal as a family–like learning to do five push-ups or finishing a book–and track progress.
- **Celebrate Mistakes:** At dinner or bedtime, share a mistake you made that day. Ask your child to share one too. Applaud the learning behind it.

Activities for All Ages

Each activity builds confidence in effort, perseverance, and problem-solving.

Babies (0–18 Months)

Why? Babies begin learning persistence through repetition and cause-and-effect play.

Activity 1: Stack and Try Again

Provide stacking cups or soft blocks. When they fall down, encourage your baby to try again, without rushing in to "fix" it for them. This repetition teaches that things don't have to go right the first time to be worth trying.

Activity 2: Try Again Song

When something drops or goes "wrong," sing a cheerful tune, "Oops! Try again, try again, you can do it!" This creates emotional safety around making mistakes and introduces persistence as playful, not stressful.

Toddlers (18 Months–3 Years)

Why? Toddlers build grit when supported through frustration rather than being rescued from it.

Activity 1: Messy Art Experiment

Set up an open-ended art station with finger paints, sponges, and brushes. Focus on the process, not the product. This allows them to explore creativity without a "right" way to do it, teaching freedom through trying.

Activity 2: You Did It! Chart

Choose a task they often resist (like brushing their teeth or putting on their shoes). Add a sticker for every attempt, not just completion. This shifts focus from success to effort, making the act of trying the thing to celebrate.

Little Kids (3–5 Years)

Why? At this age, kids may start to compare themselves to others. They need extra encouragement to keep going, especially when things feel hard.

Activity 1: Puzzle Power

Pick a puzzle that's just a little tricky. Sit with your child through the frustration. Model patience and say things like, "You're really thinking hard. That's how we grow our brains!" This builds tolerance for struggle and encourages problem-solving.

Activity 2: Famous Failures Storytime

Read picture books about real people who failed before they succeeded—like scientists, inventors, or artists. Follow up with a question: "What would've happened if they gave up?" This helps reframe setbacks as steppingstones.

Big Kids (5–13 Years)

Why? Older children benefit from visualizing their growth and rehearsing how to respond when things don't go as planned.

Activity 1: Growth Graph

Let your child pick a goal (learning to cook, doing a cartwheel, improving a test score). Track progress over time with a simple graph or chart. Seeing improvement helps anchor the idea that effort leads to change.

Activity 2: Growth Mindset Role-Play

Act out two versions of a tough moment, like failing a test or losing a game. In one version, use a fixed mindset reaction ("I'm just bad at this!"). On the other hand, show a growth response ("I'll figure out what to do next time"). Let your child try both roles. It turns abstract ideas into lived experience.

AFFIRMATION TO REINFORCE CORE BELIEFS ....

"I can do hard things.
I can pause or push through.
I trust my body and heart.
I know what to do."

Personalized Growth Mindset Plan

- How do I want my child to feel about learning and mistakes?
- What's one way I can model resilience for them?

Key takeaway:

- Success isn't about being perfect—it's about keeping going, even when it's tough.

CHAPTER 10

Self-Acceptance: Embracing Imperfection

Refer to CHAPTER 14 of **All Feelings Welcome** *for deeper learning and under-standing about this concept.*

Every parent faces moments—when your child messes up, spills something, gets frustrated, or gives up too soon—when you feel that familiar tug inside: *Should I correct them? Should I comfort them? Should I let it go?* And often, beneath those questions lies something deeper: our own story with mistakes.

Many of us grew up with the belief that being "good" meant being right, quiet, neat, successful. Perfection was praised. Mistakes were something to fix or hide. Shame often followed when we fell short. We internalized the message that love and worthiness might only be available if we measured up.

But perfectionism is a burden—one that can be passed down unintention-ally, even in loving homes. And that's why self-acceptance is such a powerful anti-dote. It's not about lowering standards or avoiding growth. It's about building the inner safety to say, "Even when I mess up, I am still worthy. Even when I struggle, I am still enough."

In *All Feelings Welcome*, we describe how self-acceptance allows children to meet their full range of experiences with compassion instead of shame. When we create space for mistakes, model grace, and separate worth from performance, we give children permission to be whole—not perfect.

Our Slumberkins character **Yak** struggles with this deeply. She tries hard, cares deeply, and wants to get it "just right." But Yak also learns that the road to confidence isn't paved with flawless effort—it's built on softness, support, and self-forgiveness.

This chapter invites you to reflect on how you've been shaped by perfec-tionism or shame—and how you can model a more compassionate relationship with imperfection, for yourself and for your child.

Let's begin.

Self-acceptance is the foundation of emotional resilience, confidence, and overall well-being. It allows children to see their worth as separate from achievements, mistakes, or external validation.

Children who develop self-acceptance build beliefs like:

"I am worthy, even when I make mistakes."

"I don't have to be perfect to be loved."

"I am enough as I am."

Without self-acceptance, children may internalize beliefs like:

"If I'm not perfect, I'm not good enough."

"Mistakes mean I have failed."

"If I don't succeed, I am unworthy."

Perfectionism is often reinforced by shame, shaped by early messages about success, discipline, or "doing things the right way." Many of us carry these messages into adulthood and parenting—without realizing it.

Self-Reflection: Your Relationship with Perfectionism and Shame

Journaling prompts:

- How was success and failure handled in my family growing up?
- Was I rewarded more for effort or for "getting it right"?
- When I make mistakes, how do I talk to myself?
- When my child struggles with something, do I rush to correct them or let them figure it out?

Perfectionism awareness check:

- I feel the need to be perfect when:

  _____

- I struggle to forgive myself when:

  _____

- One way I can practice self-acceptance is:

  _____

Reflection question:

When I make a mistake, do I treat myself with kindness—or criticism? How might that influence the way my child learns to treat themselves?

Creating Balance: Strategies Based on Your Perfectionism Patterns

If You Struggle with Perfectionism
Core Belief to Build: *"I don't have to be perfect to be loved."*

Activities to embrace imperfection:
- **Messy Art Practice:** Create something without a plan. Scribble, splash, or color outside the lines—and talk about how it felt.
- **Reframing "Failure":** Replace "I failed" with "I learned something new." Say it aloud when things go sideways.
- **The Self-Compassion Letter:** Write a letter to yourself after a hard moment as if you were comforting a dear friend. Then read it back to yourself.

If You Overemphasize Achievement in Parenting
Core Belief to Build: *"My child's worth is not based on performance."*

Activities to focus on effort, not results:
- **Praise the Process:** Shift your language to recognize effort: "I loved how you stuck with that, even when it was tricky."
- **Celebrate "Oops" Moments:** Tell stories about your own funny or awkward mistakes—and what you learned. Laugh together.
- **The "Good Enough" Challenge:** Let your child see you leave something imperfect—a crumpled bed, a mismatched outfit—and show pride anyway.

Activities for All Ages

Each activity builds confidence in imperfection and nurtures self-acceptance.

Babies (0–18 Months)

Why? Babies build trust in their worthiness through consistent, loving responses—especially during difficult moments.

Activity 1: The I Love You Ritual

At bedtime, hold your baby close and say gently: "I love you just as you are." Repetition of this message builds early emotional safety and unconditional acceptance.

Activity 2: Silly Play

Make exaggerated facial expressions, playful "mistakes," or silly sounds. Let your baby see you laugh at yourself. This models that joy doesn't require perfection, and connection comes through shared delight.

Toddlers (18 Months–3 Years)

Why? Toddlers are just beginning to notice "success" versus "failure" and may become frustrated when things go wrong.

Activity 1: Knock It Down

Build a block tower together, then knock it over on purpose. Say, "Oops! That was fun—let's do it again!" This teaches that impermanence and messiness are part of play—not signs of failure.

Activity 2: Messy Painting

Let your toddler finger paint or create without direction. Celebrate the process: "Wow, look at all those colors you chose!" This reinforces creativity over correctness.

Little Kids (3–5 Years)

Why? Kids begin comparing themselves to peers and may feel shame when they don't "measure up."

Activity 1: The Mistake Jar

Keep a jar where anyone can drop a note about a mistake they made. Once a week, read them aloud and celebrate what was learned. This makes mistakes safe to name—and something to be proud of.

Activity 2: Books About Mistakes

Read stories about characters who mess up, learn, and grow (e.g., *The Beautiful Oops!*, *Ish*). Talk about how they felt—and what helped. These stories model resilience and normalize imperfection.

Big Kids (5–13 Years)

Why? Older kids often tie their value to performance and may hide struggles to avoid judgment.

Activity 1: The Failure Résumé

Make a "résumé" listing things they tried and didn't succeed at—along with what they learned from each one. This helps reframe failure as experience and shows how growth comes from falling short.

Activity 2: Role-Playing Perfection

Act out two versions of a moment: one where a character is afraid to try, and one where they mess up and laugh it off. Talk about which one feels better—and why. This supports emotional flexibility and self-forgiveness.

AFFIRMATION TO REINFORCE CORE BELIEFS ||||||||||||||||||||||||||||||||||||||||||||||||||||||||||||||||||||

"I am enough,
just as I am.
I don't have to be perfect
to be loved."

Personalized Self-Acceptance Plan

- How can I show my child that mistakes are okay?
- How can I practice self-compassion in my own life?

Key takeaway:

- We are not meant to be perfect. We are meant to be whole.

CHAPTER 11

Conflict Resolution: Navigating Big Emotions with Confidence

Refer to CHAPTER 15 of **All Feelings Welcome** *for deeper learning and under-standing about this concept.*

Few parenting moments are as overwhelming as a child in the middle of a melt-down—or a quiet, seething stare when something doesn't go their way. Anger has a way of lighting up the nervous system, especially over something that didn't feel safe growing up. Maybe you were taught to ignore it, or were punished for express-ing it. Or perhaps you were never shown what healthy conflict even looks like.

But anger itself isn't the problem—unprocessed anger is. And most of us didn't get the tools for navigating big feelings. Instead, we were handed silence, shame, or shouting.

Conflict is part of being human. It's a natural signal that something needs attention, a boundary may be crossed, or a need has gone unmet. But how we handle it—especially in front of and with our children—sends a lasting message: *Are emotions safe here? Can I express big feelings and still be loved?*

In *All Feelings Welcome*, we explore how important it is to co-regulate emo-tions with our children. Conflict isn't something to fear or avoid—it's an opportunity to model emotional responsibility, empathy, and repair. It's in these moments, when emotions are high and patience is low, that the real learning happens—for us and for them.

Our Slumberkins character **Hammerhead** knows this well. He's fierce and full of feeling. And while his strength is clear, his journey is about learning how to use that power with care. Hammerhead reminds us that emotions like anger aren't bad—they're just signals. And when we teach our kids to listen to those signals with compassion, we help them grow into emotionally grounded, self-aware humans.

This chapter helps you unpack your own story in relation to anger and conflict—and gives you tools to support your child through big emotions with con-nection and confidence.

Let's begin.

Conflict is a normal and necessary part of relationships, yet many of us weren't taught how to handle it well. Instead, we may have learned:

- To avoid conflict completely (believing it's dangerous or damaging)
- To react explosively (because anger wasn't modeled in a healthy way)
- To suppress emotions (because expressing anger felt unsafe or unacceptable)

Children who learn healthy conflict resolution develop beliefs like:

> "My emotions are valid, even when I'm upset."
>
> "I can express anger without hurting others."
>
> "It's safe to work through conflict."

Without these skills, children may internalize beliefs like:

> "Anger is bad and should be hidden."
>
> "If I express my feelings, I will get in trouble."
>
> "Big emotions make people leave."

Supporting anger and conflict is one of the hardest challenges in parenting, because many of us have complicated relationships with anger ourselves.

Self-Reflection: Your Relationship with Anger and Conflict

Journaling prompts:
- How was anger handled in my home growing up? Was it safe to express?
- When I get angry, do I suppress it, explode, or express it in a balanced way?
- Do I view conflict as something to avoid, win, or work through?
- What do I feel when my child is angry? Does it trigger stress, fear, or a need to control the situation?

Conflict awareness check:

- I feel most uncomfortable when conflict is:

  _____

- My first instinct in an argument is to:

  _____

- One way I can support anger in a healthy way is:

  _____

Reflection question:

When someone is angry with me, what do I believe that says about me? How might that belief show up in the way I respond to my child's anger?

Creating Balance: Strategies Based on Your Conflict Style

If You Tend to Avoid Conflict (Suppressing Anger)
Core Belief to Build: *"I can handle conflict without fear."*

Activities to embrace emotional expression:
- **The "I Feel" Rule:** Start by naming one feeling out loud each day. This makes emotional expression a habit, not a risk.
- **Practice Small Conflicts:** Role-play tiny disagreements (e.g., what to have for dinner) to make conflict feel less threatening.
- **Anger Is Allowed:** When your child is mad, say out loud: "It's okay to be mad. Let's figure out what to do with that feeling." This gives permission *and* a path forward.

If You React Strongly to Conflict (Explosive or Defensive Responses)
Core Belief to Build: *"I can express anger without hurting others."*

Activities to regulate emotions in conflict:
- **Pause Before Reacting:** When emotions rise, take three deep breaths before speaking. Step away if needed.
- **Physical Release:** Try shaking out your hands, jumping in place, or stomping to let energy move out of the body safely. Invite your child to do it too.

- **The Repair Process:** If you react harshly, name it and model repair: "I got too loud. I'm sorry. I want to do that better." Repair is where healing and trust are built.

....

Activities for All Ages

Each activity helps children express anger safely and resolve conflicts with confidence.

Babies (0–18 Months)

Why? Infants begin learning emotional safety through how caregivers respond to distress.

Activity 1: Calm Voice, Safe Arms

When your baby is crying or upset, hold them and use a slow, soothing voice: "I hear you. I'm right here." This models co-regulation and builds a foundation of trust during heightened emotion.

Activity 2: Gentle Touch

Gently stroke your baby's arm or back and say, "Your feelings are safe with me." This simple phrase introduces emotional acceptance before language even develops.

Toddlers (18 Months–3 Years)

Why? Toddlers need simple, physical ways to express anger safely.

Activity 1: Stomp It Out

When your child feels frustrated, invite them to stomp like a dinosaur or march like in a parade. This provides a safe outlet for big energy and shows that movement can help shift emotion.

Activity 2: Anger Scribbles

Offer crayons or chalk and a big piece of paper. Say, "Let's scribble all those mad feelings!" Then rip it up together. This gives a visual, physical way to release emotion and feel completion.

Little Kids (3–5 Years)

Why? Kids at this stage need language, tools, and permission to express hard feelings.

Activity 1: The Mad Box

Create a kit with pillows to punch, paper to tear, or squishy balls to squeeze. Let your child know: "This is your space to feel mad safely." The presence of a "mad box" teaches containment, not suppression.

Activity 2: Face the Feelings

Look in the mirror together and make angry, sad, and frustrated faces. Name the feelings: "This is what mad looks like. And mad is okay." This builds emotional literacy and normalizes facial expressions of emotion.

Big Kids (5–13 Years)

Why? Older kids need tools to self-regulate, reflect, and communicate during conflict.

Activity 1: The Anger Scale

Create a 1–10 scale to help your child check in before reacting. Ask, "How mad are you right now?" Use it to pause and plan their next step. This builds self-awareness and a habit of internal check-ins.

Activity 2: Conflict Role-Play

Practice common challenges like a sibling disagreement or feeling left out. Explore both healthy and hurtful ways to respond, then talk about the differences. This gives them a rehearsal space for real-life emotional moments.

"I felt mad, now I'm calm.
I can use my words instead.
I'm sorry I hurt you,
I still want to be friends."

Personalized Conflict Resolution Plan

- How can I show my child that anger is okay, but aggression is not?
- What's one new way I can approach conflict in my family?

Key takeaway:

- Anger is not the enemy—unprocessed anger is. Learning how to handle big emotions is one of the most powerful life skills we can give our children.

CHAPTER 12

Change: Navigating the Uncontrollable

Refer to CHAPTER 16 of All Feelings Welcome *for deeper learning and understanding about this concept.*

Change is one of the few things we can count on in life—and one of the hardest to accept, especially for children. Whether it's a move, a new school, a new sibling, or a shift in family dynamics, change often arrives without their permission or preparation. And when children feel powerless, their inner world fills in the blanks. *Did I cause this? Did I do something wrong?*

Many of us can relate. Maybe change in your own childhood wasn't talked about. Maybe you learned to brace yourself, to stay quiet, to push forward instead of processing. Maybe you still feel tension or resistance when things shift, even when you know they're "for the best."

In *All Feelings Welcome*, we talk about how children are naturally egocentric in their early development—they see the world as revolving around them. So when something breaks, ends, or moves on, they often think it's their fault. *If I had been better. . . . If I hadn't cried. . . . Maybe they'd still be here.*

This is why our response matters so much. The way we show up during transitions helps shape the way our children understand themselves in the world. Not just whether they're safe, but whether they can *handle* change without shame or fear.

Our Slumberkins character **Fox** was created for these moments. Fox is the brave guide through big transitions—separation, family changes, or new beginnings. Fox doesn't pretend change is easy. But he shows children that they're not alone in it, that it's okay to grieve, and that there's always a thread of connection they can hold on to, even when things feel uncertain.

This chapter is here to help you hold that thread with your child. Whether the change is big or small, expected or sudden, we can help our children build the belief that *change is not their fault—and they are never alone in it.*

Let's begin.

Change is inevitable. From a child's perspective, most change happens outside of their control—moving homes, starting school, the arrival of a new sibling, or changes in family structure like divorce.

Because of their developmental stage, children often internalize change as personal:

> *"If I had been better, this wouldn't have happened."*
> *"I must have done something wrong."*
> *"I should have tried harder."*

Without guidance, these misunderstandings can become lasting negative core beliefs about control and self-worth.

Children who learn to navigate change with support develop beliefs like:

> *"Change is hard, but I can handle it."*
> *"I am not responsible for everything that happens around me."*
> *"Even when things change, I am still safe and loved."*

Self-Reflection: Your Relationship with Change and Control

Journaling prompts:

- How was change handled in my family growing up? Was it talked about openly or avoided?
- Did I feel like I had control over my own life as a child?
- When change happens in my life now, do I embrace it, resist it, or feel anxious?
- How do I react when my child struggles with change? Do I try to fix it quickly, minimize their feelings, or allow them space to process?

Change awareness check:

- I feel most resistant to change when:

  _____

- I feel most in control when:

  _____

- One way I can model adaptability for my child is:

  _____

Reflection question:

What story did I learn about change growing up—and how might that story be shaping the way I help (or avoid helping) my child navigate it?

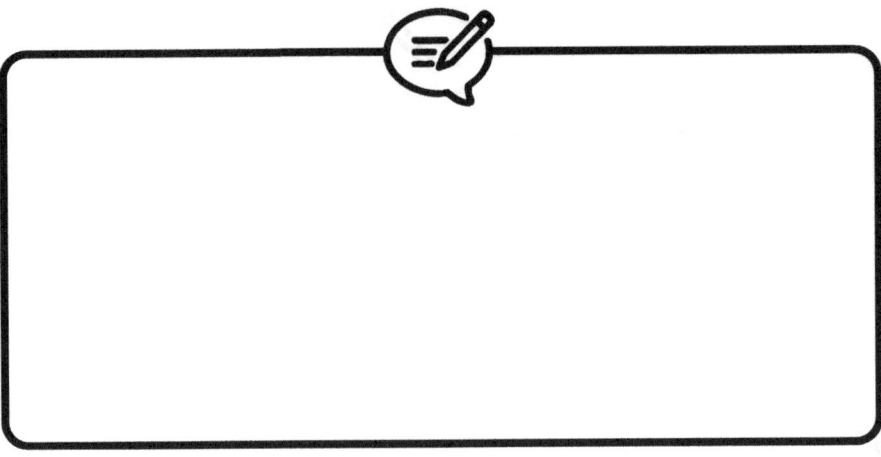

Creating Balance: Strategies Based on Your Change Patterns

If You Struggle with Control (Wanting Stability and Predictability)
Core Belief to Build: *"I can find steadiness even when things change."*

Activities to build adaptability:
- **The "What If" Game:** Playfully explore outcomes together: "What if our new neighbor has a dog that loves belly rubs?"
- **Create Small, Safe Changes:** Try something new together in a low-stakes way—like eating dinner on a picnic blanket. Talk about what it felt like to change things up.
- **Name a Constant:** When something shifts, anchor your child by highlighting what's staying the same: "We'll be in a new house, but your bedtime songs will always be with you."

If You Tend to Avoid Talking About Change (Minimizing or Distracting)
Core Belief to Build: *"I can face change openly and honestly."*

Activities to increase comfort with change:
- **Tell "Change Stories":** Share a time when a change was hard for you—and what helped you through it.
- **The Transition Calendar:** When a big change is coming, create a visual count-down to help your child prepare. Include feelings check-ins along the way.
- **Validate, Don't Fix:** Swap "It's not a big deal" for "This is really hard. I'm right here with you." Let your presence be the comfort, not the solution.

Activities for All Ages

Each activity helps children process and navigate change in a healthy way.

Babies (0–18 Months)

Why? Babies need predictability and comfort when surroundings shift.

Activity 1: Safe Routines

Keep one familiar routine steady (a bedtime song, bath ritual, or feeding spot) during transitions like moving or travel. This provides an anchor of security when everything else feels unfamiliar.

Activity 2: Comfort Object

Offer a consistent item—a soft blanket, a parent's shirt, or a favorite lovey—when something changes. This helps babies associate emotional safety with something they can touch and hold.

Toddlers (18 Months–3 Years)

Why? Toddlers thrive on routine but benefit from gentle exposure to change.

Activity 1: New and Old Box

Place familiar items in one box (labeled "Old") and new ones (like a new baby's toy or item from a new house) in another. Explore both together. This helps them visually and emotionally process that "new" and "old" can coexist.

Activity 2: Goodbye Ritual

Create a small ceremony when saying goodbye to something, like waving to the old house or hugging a toy that's being donated. This gives closure and honors what's changing without rushing past it.

Little Kids (3–5 Years)

Why? Kids this age often believe change is their fault and need help naming their feelings.

Activity 1: The River of Change

Draw a river with stepping stones. On each stone, write one thing that's changing—and one thing that's staying the same. This builds perspective and reminds them that not everything changes at once.

Activity 2: Feelings Puppet Show

Use stuffed animals or puppets to act out fears or sadness about change. Let your child guide the story. This gives them emotional distance while still expressing their inner world.

Big Kids (5–13 Years)

Why? Older children are developing a more nuanced understanding of time and need tools to reflect and look ahead.

Activity 1: My Change Timeline

Invite your child to create a timeline of past changes in their life. Write down what happened and what they learned or felt afterward. This builds emotional resilience and reminds them of their ability to adapt.

Activity 2: Letter to My Future Self

Have them write a letter about what they're feeling now and what they hope or imagine in six months. Set a reminder to open it later. This fosters long-term thinking and self-compassion during tough transitions.

AFFIRMATION TO REINFORCE CORE BELIEFS ••

"I am safe, I am loved.
I can get through this part.
It is not my fault that things changed,
and I can keep an open heart."

Personalized Change Plan

- How can I help my child understand that change is not their fault?
- What's one way I can model handling change with honesty and openness?

Key takeaway:

- Change is part of life. What matters most is how we guide our children through it.

CHAPTER 13

Anxiety: Finding Calm in the Unknown

Refer to CHAPTER 17 of **All Feelings Welcome** *for deeper learning and understanding about this concept.*

Anxiety doesn't always show up how we expect. Sometimes it's a racing mind. Sometimes it's a stomachache before school. Sometimes it's anger, perfectionism, or needing to control everything—because underneath, something feels out of place.

For parents, watching a child struggle with worry can stir up deep responses. We might try to soothe too quickly. We might shut it down, hoping it passes. Or we might feel helpless—especially if we never learned what to do with anxiety ourselves.

In *All Feelings Welcome*, we talk about anxiety as the brain's built-in alarm system. It's there to keep us safe. But without tools to understand and manage it, that alarm can get stuck on—leaving kids overwhelmed, afraid to try, or convinced that something bad is always just around the corner.

The way we respond to worry—our own and our children's—shapes the story they tell themselves about safety and control. Do I have to fix everything to feel okay? Or can I face hard things with support?

Our Slumberkins character **Alpaca** was created for moments like these. Alpaca doesn't have all the answers. But he knows how to carry heavy feelings with compassion. He reminds us that we don't have to handle everything alone—and that asking for help is brave.

This chapter helps you support your child through worry and uncertainty—not by fixing it all, but by helping them break it down, find what they can control, and let go of what they can't. Because peace doesn't come from eliminating fear. It comes from learning that we can move through it—together.

Let's begin.

Anxiety isn't always bad. It's the brain's internal alarm—helping us stay safe and prepared. But when anxiety is left unchecked, it can become overwhelming and lead to avoidance or distress.

Children who learn to process anxiety develop beliefs like:

> *"I can feel worry and still take action."*
> *"Not everything is in my control, and that's okay."*
> *"I can calm my body and mind when I feel overwhelmed."*

Without tools to manage anxiety, children may internalize beliefs like:

> *"I have to control everything to feel safe."*
> *"Worry means something bad is about to happen."*
> *"If I can't fix it, I'm powerless."*

Helping children break down anxiety into manageable parts teaches them the difference between control and surrender—and how to trust themselves through uncertainty.

Self-Reflection: Your Relationship with Anxiety and Control

Journaling prompts:

- When I feel anxious, do I try to control, avoid, or overthink the situation?
- Growing up, was anxiety something we talked about, or was I expected to "push through"?
- How do I react when my child expresses worry? Do I try to fix it, dismiss it, or co-regulate with them?
- What areas of my life currently cause me anxiety? How might these be markers for self-care needs?

Anxiety awareness check:

- I tend to worry most about:

  _____

- I try to control things when:

  _____

- One way I can practice releasing worry is:

  _____

Reflection question:

When something feels out of my control, how do I respond—and what might that teach my child about uncertainty?

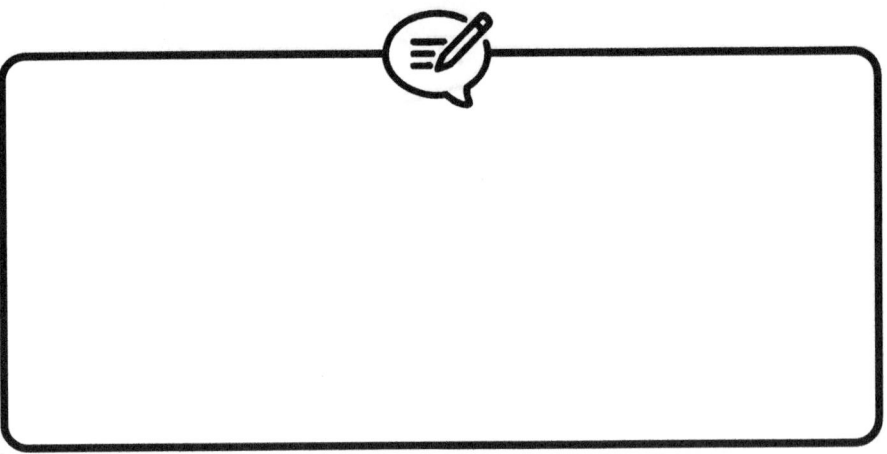

Breaking Down Anxiety: Strategies for Managing Worry

Step 1: identify what can be controlled, versus what needs to be released.
Activity: The "Three Circles of Control"
Draw three circles:

- **Inner Circle:** What I *can* control (my thoughts, my actions, my breathing)
- **Middle Circle:** What I *can influence* (preparation, how I communicate)
- **Outer Circle:** What I *cannot* control (others' choices, big life events)

Invite your child to place their worries in each circle. This creates clarity and a sense of empowerment.

Step 2: Create a plan for what you can control.
Activity: The "First-Step" List
If a worry falls in the Inner or Middle Circle, ask, "What's one small thing we can do today?" This helps shift focus from overwhelm to action.

Step 3: Release the worries you cannot control.
Activity: "Worry Release Ritual"

Write or draw worries that belong in the Outer Circle and choose one of the following:

- Tear them up and throw them away.
- Place them in a "Worry Jar."
- Imagine tying them to a balloon and letting them float away.

This teaches that not every worry needs fixing—and some can simply be released.

Spirituality and Meaning-Making: Navigating the Unimaginable

Sometimes anxiety is rooted in loss, illness, or events that are truly out of our hands. In those moments, we turn to the deeper tools—faith, nature, ritual, story. How we make sense of the hard stuff shapes what our children believe about life, safety, and meaning.

Children trying to process tragedy may believe:
> *"This happened because I was bad."*
> *"The world is unpredictable, so I should always be afraid."*
> *"Nothing I love will stay."*

To support them, we can:
- **Acknowledge the unknown:** "I don't have all the answers, but I'm here with you."
- **Offer a meaning-making framework:** Religious or spiritual beliefs, nature-based metaphors, or family wisdom.
- **Let grief and wonder coexist:** It's okay to hold sadness and beauty in the same breath.

Activity: "The Circle of Life" Discussion
Talk about how things change, but continue—seasons, stars, traditions.

Ask: *"What are some things that stay the same, even when other things change?"*
This helps children explore impermanence in a way that feels gentle and safe.

Activities for All Ages

Each activity helps children recognize, process, and release anxiety in an age-appropriate way.

Babies (0–18 Months)

Why? Babies co-regulate through their caregivers' breath, presence, and rhythm.

Activity 1: Calm Heart, Calm Baby

Hold your baby close, chest to chest, and breathe slowly. Over time, their body will sync to yours. This builds foundational safety through nervous system connection.

Activity 2: Soothing Sounds

Repeat a calming phrase like "I am here, and you are safe" during diaper changes, bedtime, or transitions. This anchors comfort in your voice and predictability.

Toddlers (18 Months–3 Years)

Why? Toddlers are sensitive to changes in routine and benefit from rhythmic, sensory coping tools.

Activity 1: The Worry Song

Create a silly, rhythmic tune to sing when your child is worried. For example: "Worries, worries, go away–we can talk another day!" This helps to externalize anxiety through play.

Activity 2: Safe Hands

Invite them to press their palms into yours when they're upset. Breathe together. This grounding technique creates safety through sensory input and connection.

Little Kids (3–5 Years)

Why? Children this age are developing emotional language and benefit from visualizing their worries.

Activity 1: The Worry Box

Create and decorate a small box. When a worry comes up, help your child draw or write it down and place it inside. This gives the worry a place to go–and helps them learn containment.

Activity 2: Bravery Superhero

Make a superhero costume or badge and name their "calm powers." This helps reframe anxiety through imagination and empowerment.

Big Kids (5–13 Years)

Why? Older kids can learn reflective techniques and grounding tools for long-term use.

Activity 1: Anxiety Journal

Encourage your child to write about their worries and pair each with either one small action or one way to let go. This balances reflection with emotional movement.

Activity 2: The Five Senses Reset

Guide your child through a grounding technique:

- Five things you see
- Four things you can touch
- Three things you hear
- Two things you smell
- One thing you taste

This brings their awareness back to the present moment, especially helpful during panic or spiraling thoughts.

AFFIRMATION TO REINFORCE CORE BELIEFS ···

"I am strong and supported.
I am never alone.
Climbing these mountains
will lead me home."

Key takeaways:

- **Anxiety is a messenger, not a mandate.** When worry shows up, our job is to *listen*, decide what is and isn't in our control, and choose a next step.
- **Feelings get lighter when they're shared.** Alpaca teaches that speaking a fear out loud (or whispering it into a plush ear) immediately reduces its intensity and invites support.
- **Small actions shift big feelings.** One slow breath, one grounding phrase, or one "first-step" task is often enough to flip the nervous-system switch from alarm to calm.
- **Control and surrender are partners.** Kids can learn, "I handle what's mine and release what isn't." This builds flexible, realistic confidence.
- **Bravery looks quiet.** Asking for help, choosing rest, or trying again tomorrow are all courageous responses to anxiety.

CHAPTER 14

Grief and Loss: Holding Space for Big Feelings

Refer to CHAPTER 18 of All Feelings Welcome *for deeper learning and understanding about this concept.*

Grief is one of the hardest things we feel—and one of the most important to talk about. Yet so many of us grew up without the tools to do that. Maybe when someone died, no one explained it. Maybe you were told to "be strong" or that your sadness made things harder for others. Maybe you learned to hold your feelings quietly because you thought they weren't okay to share.

But grief needs space. It needs slowness, honesty, and comfort. It needs room to revisit old memories, ask big questions, and simply *feel*—without being rushed to "move on."

In *All Feelings Welcome*, we remind families that children process grief differently at different ages—and often in waves. A child might seem "fine" one moment, and deeply sad the next. They may ask the same question again and again, not because they forgot, but because they're trying to understand something their brain and heart aren't yet ready to fully hold.

Our Slumberkins character **Sprite** was created for these moments. Sprite doesn't offer quick fixes or false promises. Instead, they offer presence, comfort, and a safe space for all feelings—grief, love, confusion, wonder. Sprite reminds us that loss is real, but love doesn't disappear. It continues in memories, in rituals, in the stories we carry forward.

This chapter will help you explore your own beliefs about loss, guide honest conversations with your child, and create simple, meaningful rituals for remembering. Because grief doesn't end—it changes. And our role as parents isn't to make it go away, but to walk alongside it, together.

Let's begin.

Grief is an unavoidable part of life, yet many of us were not taught how to process it openly.

Instead, we may have received messages like:

"Be strong." This can lead to emotional suppression.

"Time heals all wounds." This can create pressure to "move on" quickly.

"They're in a better place." While comforting to some, this may minimize real pain.

Children who are supported through grief develop beliefs like:

"It's okay to be sad, and I don't have to hide my feelings."

"Love doesn't go away, even when someone is gone."

"I can carry memories with me while still moving forward."

Without support, children may internalize beliefs like:

"I shouldn't talk about my feelings."

"If I cry, I'm making others uncomfortable."

"Everything I love will leave."

Children revisit loss as they grow. A child who loses a loved one at age five may grieve again in a new way at 10, when their understanding of death deepens. Grief is not one moment—it's a relationship that evolves.

Self-Reflection: Your Relationship with Grief

Journaling prompts:

- What messages did I receive about grief growing up?
- Have I ever felt pressure to "move on" before I was ready?
- How do I process loss—through talking, solitude, distraction?
- How do I feel when my child is deeply sad? Do I try to fix it, change the subject, or hold space?

Grief awareness check:

- I feel most uncomfortable with grief when:

  _____

- I was taught that loss should be handled by:

  _____

- One way I can model healthy grieving is:

  _____

Reflection question:

When my child expresses sadness, what do I feel responsible for—fixing their pain, or walking through it with them?

Talking About Grief: Honest Conversations Without Fear

Adults often feel unsure of what to say when a child experiences loss. In trying to protect them, we may use vague or confusing language:

⊘ *"Grandpa went to sleep."* This can create a fear of sleep.

⊘ *"We lost the dog."* This may lead children to believe they just need to find them.

☑ Instead, use clear, age-appropriate language:

"Grandpa died. That means his body stopped working, and we won't see him anymore. But we can always remember him."
"Our pet died. We feel sad because we loved them, and it's okay to miss them."

These honest conversations build core beliefs like:
"Grief is not something to be afraid of."
"It's okay to talk about people we miss."
"I don't have to pretend I'm okay."

Activities for All Ages

Each activity helps children process grief in age-appropriate ways while reinforcing connection and comfort.

Babies (0–18 Months)

Why? Babies sense emotional shifts even if they don't understand loss.

Activity 1: The Comfort Carry

Hold or wear your baby close, especially during emotional times. Your steady presence and slow breathing regulate their nervous system. This tells them: *You're safe, even when things feel different*.

Activity 2: Lullaby of Love

Sing a familiar song associated with the loved one. It becomes a comforting thread between memory and presence.

Toddlers (18 Months–3 Years)

Why? Toddlers don't understand permanence, so repetition and reassurance are key.

Activity 1: Memory Drawing

Invite them to draw their loved one or pet. When they ask where that person is, say: "They aren't here anymore, but we can remember them anytime we want." This builds understanding and connection.

Activity 2: Planting Memories

Plant a flower, tree, or herb in honor of someone. Talk about how love can keep growing, even when someone is gone. This creates a ritual of remembrance they can revisit.

Little Kids (3–5 Years)

Why? Children at this age may believe they caused the loss. They need reassurance and symbolic closure.

Activity 1: Letters to Heaven

Help your child draw or write a message to someone they miss. Place it in a keep-sake box or burn it safely as a ritual. This gives them a tangible way to express love and release emotions.

Activity 2: A Goodbye Ritual

If a pet or person dies, create a small ceremony: light a candle, share memories, and say goodbye together. This helps children process and feel closure with support.

Big Kids (5–13 Years)

Why? Older children begin asking big questions and need space for emotional exploration.

Activity 1: The Memory Book

Create a scrapbook or journal with photos, drawings, and stories about the loved one. Add to it over time. This helps preserve the relationship and provides a safe outlet for grief.

Activity 2: What Would They Say?

Ask, "If [person] could talk to you right now, what do you think they'd say?" This supports emotional connection even in absence—and can be deeply comforting.

Spirituality and Meaning-Making: Finding Comfort in the Unknown

Grief often brings up big questions: *"Why do people die? What happens next?"* Children don't need all the answers. What they need is safety to wonder, space to feel, and the comfort of knowing they're not alone in their questions.

Ways to support meaning-making:

- **If your family has spiritual beliefs:** Share them gently as comfort, and allow for questions.
- **If your family is nonreligious:** Use nature metaphors, *"Just like leaves fall, and new ones grow, everything has a cycle."*
- **Encourage wonder, not just answers:** *"No one knows exactly what happens, but what do you think? What do you hope?"*

Core belief to reinforce:

> *"We don't have to have all the answers to feel love and connection."*

> **"Though today is hard,**
> **I am going to start.**
> **The journey ahead,**
> **with you in my heart."**

Personalized Grief Support Plan

- How can I help my child feel safe expressing sadness?
- What's one way I can honor my own grief process?

Key takeaway:

- Grief isn't about moving on—it's about carrying love forward.

CHAPTER 15

Self-Expression and Boundaries: The Power of Your Voice

Refer to CHAPTER 19 of **All Feelings Welcome** *for deeper learning and understanding about this concept.*

There's something deeply powerful about watching a child speak up—whether it's a quiet "no," a proud "I did it," or a strong "I don't like that." In these moments, children aren't just expressing themselves—they're building a belief that their voice matters, and their body belongs to them.

Many of us didn't grow up with that message. Maybe we were told to "be polite," even when something felt uncomfortable. Maybe we learned that saying no would get us in trouble, or that disagreeing meant disrespect. For some, expressing a boundary felt dangerous, or wasn't modeled at all.

In *All Feelings Welcome*, we explore how honoring our children's voices—especially when they say no or express discomfort—is one of the most important ways we can build their inner compass. It's how we teach them they have the right to be heard, to be safe, and to trust their own instincts.

Our Slumberkins character **Lynx** reminds us that self-expression isn't about being loud—it's about being true. Lynx shows kids that they can speak up and still be kind. That they can disagree and still be connected. That they can express a boundary without fear of losing love.

This chapter helps you reflect on your own history with self-expression and boundaries, and gives you tools to raise a child who knows how to use their voice—not just for confidence, but for safety, resilience, and self-respect.

Let's begin.

Self-expression and personal boundaries go hand in hand. Teaching children to use their voice is not just about speaking up—it's about recognizing their right to:

- Be heard
- Say no
- Protect their personal space and emotions

Children who develop these skills form beliefs like:

> *"My feelings and opinions matter."*
> *"I can say no if something doesn't feel right."*
> *"I am allowed to take up space and express my needs."*

Without these tools, children may internalize beliefs like:

> *"I shouldn't upset others by saying no."*
> *"Adults are always right, even if I feel uncomfortable."*
> *"If I speak up, people won't like me."*

These early beliefs don't just shape communication. They shape self-worth and vulnerability to manipulation or abuse. That's why starting early, and continuing often, is essential.

Self-Reflection: Your Relationship with Self-Expression and Boundaries

Journaling prompts:

- As a child, was I encouraged to express emotions, or told to be quiet, polite, or agreeable?
- How do I feel when my child says "no" to me? Do I respect it, push back, or feel triggered?
- When I feel uncomfortable, do I speak up or stay silent to avoid conflict?
- Have I ignored my own boundaries to keep the peace?

Boundary awareness check:

- I feel most uncomfortable setting boundaries when:

_____

- I struggle with self-expression when:

_____

- One way I can model healthy boundaries is:

_____

Reflection question:

What did I learn about saying "no" growing up—and how does that shape the way I respond when my child says it to me?

Teaching Children That Their Body and Voice Belong to Them

Step 1: Give permission to say no (even to adults).
Activity: When It's Okay to Say No

- **Ask:** *"Can you say no if someone asks for a hug?"*
- **Affirm:** *"Yes, you can always say no to touch, even from family."* This helps separate kindness from compliance–and builds the foundation for consent.

Step 2: Practice assertive communication.
Activity: Stop, Walk, Talk
Teach the three-step response for uncomfortable situations:

- **Stop:** Say *"no"* or *"I don't like that."*
- **Walk:** Move away if you can.
- **Talk:** Tell a trusted adult.

Practice together using real-life scenarios (someone takes a toy, teases, or makes them feel unsafe).

Step 3: Reinforce that secrets about bodies are never okay.
Activity: Safe versus Unsafe Secrets Game

Compare different types of secrets:

- **Safe:** *"We're throwing a surprise party!"*
- **Unsafe:** *"Don't tell anyone what happened."*

Reinforce:

> *"No one should ever ask you to keep a secret about touching or bodies."*

Core belief to reinforce:

> *"I can trust my feelings. If something feels wrong, I don't have to keep it a secret."*

....

Activities for All Ages

Each activity helps children strengthen their voice, build confidence, and trust their instincts.

Babies (0–18 Months)

Why? Babies begin learning emotional communication through caregiver responsiveness.

Activity 1: Mirror My Feelings

When your baby makes a sound or face, mirror it back and name it: "You're showing me a big feeling!" This validates their earliest expressions and builds emotional safety.

Activity 2: Pause for Consent

Before picking them up, say, "I'm going to pick you up now." Pause, even briefly. This helps them begin associating care with consent and respect.

Toddlers (18 Months–3 Years)

Why? Toddlers are learning independence and need safe opportunities to say "no."

Activity 1: No Means No Practice

Play a game where your toddler says *"NO!"* in different tones. Celebrate their use of voice. This builds comfort with assertiveness.

Activity 2: Ask Before Touching

Before hugs or tickles, ask: "Would you like a hug, high five, or something else?" This teaches everyday bodily autonomy through positive interactions.

Little Kids (3–5 Years)

Why? Preschoolers need direct language for setting boundaries and understanding emotions.

Activity 1: Use Your Strong Voice

Role-play using a firm tone to say, "Stop!" or "I don't like that." Reinforce that strong doesn't mean mean–it means clear.

Activity 2: How Does This Feel?

Act out scenes like someone taking a toy without asking. Ask, "Did that feel good or not good?" This helps connect physical responses to emotional boundaries.

Big Kids (5–13 Years)

Why? Older kids face peer pressure and need support in developing personal and emotional autonomy.

Activity 1: Assertive versus Aggressive versus Passive Game

Role-play the same scenario (e.g., someone asks them to do something uncomfortable) in three different ways. Debrief what each approach felt like and when assertiveness is most powerful.

Activity 2: Personal Boundaries Journal

Invite your child to reflect on a time they felt uncomfortable. What did they do–or wish they had done? This creates space for growth without judgment.

"My body is mine,
I know what I like.
I check in with myself
and say what feels right."

Personalized Self-Expression and Boundary Plan

- How can I help my child feel safe setting boundaries with adults and peers?
- What's one way I can model self-expression in my own life?

Key takeaway:

- Teaching children to express themselves and set boundaries is not just about confidence—it's about safety.

CHAPTER 16

Creativity: Expanding Possibilities and Problem-Solving

Refer to CHAPTER 20 of **All Feelings Welcome** *for deeper learning and understanding about this concept.*

Creativity isn't just about drawing, painting, or building something impressive. It's about the courage to try. The willingness to imagine. The curiosity to ask, *What if we did it differently?*

So often, we think of creativity as a talent—something some people are born with. But in *All Feelings Welcome*, we talk about creativity as a mindset. It's a way of being present, flexible, and open to new possibilities. It's what helps us solve problems, build emotional resilience, and stay hopeful—even when things don't go according to plan.

Many of us weren't raised to value creativity as a life skill. Maybe structure was prioritized over exploration. Maybe you were praised for getting it "right," but not for coloring outside the lines. Maybe creativity was labeled "silly" or "impractical"—and somewhere along the way, you started believing that trying something new wasn't worth the risk of getting it wrong.

But creativity is how children learn to trust their ideas. It's how they rehearse real-life problem-solving. It's how they find joy in the unknown. And when they're free to explore without fear of failure, they're also learning that there's never just *one* right way to do things.

Our Slumberkins character **Dragon** represents this magical mindset. Dragon doesn't follow the rules just to get the gold star. Dragon forges new paths. They make up songs, dream up stories, and remind children that imagination *is* wisdom— and trying something new is always worth celebrating.

This chapter invites you to reflect on your relationship with creativity and how you can create more space for it—at home, in your parenting, and in your child's life.

Let's begin.

Creativity is more than artistic skill—it's a way of thinking, problem-solving, and engaging with the world. When children are encouraged to create freely, they build self-trust, emotional flexibility, and the ability to adapt when things don't go as planned.

Children who embrace creativity develop beliefs like:

"There's always more than one way to solve a problem."

"I can trust my ideas and imagination."

"Mistakes can lead to something new."

Without creative freedom, children may internalize beliefs like:

"There is only one right way to do things."

"If I don't do it perfectly, I shouldn't even try."

"Being different is bad."

Self-Reflection: Your Relationship with Creativity

Journaling prompts:

- Was creativity encouraged in my family growing up, or was practicality valued more?
- Do I allow myself to explore or play without needing to get it "right"?
- How do I react when my child makes a mess or does something differently than expected?
- Do I see myself as a creative person—or do I believe creativity is for "other people"?

Creativity awareness check:

- I feel most creative when I:

  _____

- I struggle with creativity when:

  _____

- One way I can model creative thinking for my child is:

  _____

Reflection question:

What core belief do I carry about creativity and problem-solving—and is it one I want to pass on?

Encouraging a Growth-Oriented, Creative Mindset

Step 1: Shift focus from the end product to the process.
Activity: The Messy Middle
When working on a project with your child, pause in the middle and say, "This is the fun part–the figuring it out." This helps them find joy in experimentation, not just in getting to the "perfect" result.

Step 2: Celebrate thinking outside the box.
Activity: How Else Could We Do This?
When faced with a challenge (spilled milk, a broken toy), brainstorm together: "What are three other ways we could solve this?" This teaches flexibility and the belief that creativity lives in everyday moments.

Step 3: Reframe mistakes as part of creativity.
Activity: The Oops-to-Opportunity Game
When something goes wrong–paint spills, a tower collapses–ask, "What could we turn this into?" This helps children see that mistakes are not dead ends, but beginnings.

Core belief to reinforce:
> *"Creativity is about exploring, not getting it perfect."*

Activities for All Ages

Each activity supports exploration, imagination, and flexible problem-solving.

Babies (0–18 Months)

Why? Babies explore creativity through sensory discovery and repetition.

Activity 1: Texture Time

Let your baby explore objects with different textures–fuzzy, bumpy, smooth, crinkly. Narrate what they're experiencing. This early play builds curiosity and sensory confidence.

Activity 2: Silly Sound Play

Make up nonsense songs, playful noises, and funny tones together. This shows them that creativity can start with sound—and connection.

Toddlers (18 Months–3 Years)

Why? Toddlers love exploring pretend play and turning everyday items into magical tools.

Activity 1: Magic Object

Pick a household item and pretend it's something else. A spoon becomes a microphone. A box becomes a car. This boosts flexible thinking and symbolic play.

Activity 2: No Rules Art

Offer paint, crayons, or stickers with zero instructions. Let the mess happen. This gives your child space to express without fear of judgment.

Little Kids (3–5 Years)

Why? Pretend play and storytelling thrive in this stage—helping kids explore "what if" thinking.

Activity 1: The Anything Box

Hand your child an empty box and ask, "What could this be?" Let them transform it however they choose. This encourages divergent thinking and open-ended creativity.

Activity 2: Mix and Match Storytelling

Take turns making up a silly story—one sentence at a time. Let it be wild and weird. This builds improvisation skills and emotional flexibility.

Big Kids (5–13 Years)

Why? Older kids begin tying creativity to identity and benefit from inventive challenges.

Activity 1: Invent Something New

Gather random household items and challenge your child to invent something–useful or silly. This reinforces problem-solving and sparks innovation.

Activity 2: Act It Out

Have them act out a scene silently while others guess what it is. This strengthens expressive confidence, empathy, and creative thinking.

"I know deep inside,
I can create what I feel.
When I enter my dream world,
I can make anything real."

Personalized Creativity Plan

- How can I help my child feel safe exploring and trying new things?
- What's one way I can bring more creativity into my own life?

Key takeaway:

• Creativity is not about talent—it's about exploration, expression, and the courage to try something new.

CHAPTER 17

Final Section: Bringing It All Together

If you've made it here, take a breath—and know that you've done something extraordinary.

You've carved out time to pause, reflect, and learn—not just about your child's emotional growth, but about your own. You've looked inward, revisited childhood stories, made space for new beliefs, and embraced tools to help your family grow with more compassion and connection. That's brave work. That's meaningful work. And most importantly, that's enough.

Parenting with emotional awareness is not about always knowing what to do. It's about returning—to presence, to intention, to love—again and again, especially when it's hard. It's about sitting with discomfort, finding new language, and trying again after messy moments.

Every single time you pause to connect with your child instead of control, every time you choose repair over reaction, you are changing the story—not just for them, but for generations to come.

In *All Feelings Welcome*, we often say that parenting is less about perfection and more about pattern-breaking. It's about showing up differently than you were shown. It's about learning as you go and modeling that for your child, so they know that growth is not just for kids—it's for all of us.

This section is your invitation to take what you've learned and make it your own. You don't have to use every strategy or remember every phrase. Instead, return to what felt grounding, what made your shoulders drop, what made your heart soften. That's the path. Follow it gently.

Let this be a place to honor your work, celebrate your growth, and create a path forward that feels sustainable, meaningful, and rooted in love.

You're not alone in this journey. And you're doing better than you think. Let's reflect, integrate, and carry the most important pieces forward—together.

Reflecting on the Journey

Through these pages, you've explored:

- ☑ Your own core beliefs and how they shape your parenting
- ☑ Ways to connect with your child through routines, mindfulness, and self-expression
- ☑ How to help your child develop positive core beliefs about themselves and the world
- ☑ Practical strategies for emotional regulation, conflict resolution, and navigating big emotions

This journey wasn't just about teaching your child; it was about unlearning what no longer serves you and making space for a different way—a softer, braver, more connected way.

Reflection questions:

- What has been the most powerful insight I've gained about myself as a parent?
- Which core belief from this workbook resonated most deeply with me?
- Where do I still feel challenged in supporting my child's emotional growth?

Journaling prompt:

Write a letter to yourself. What have you learned? What do you want to remember on hard days? What kind of parent are you becoming—and what do you want to keep believing about yourself?

Creating a Personalized Emotional Growth Plan

You don't need to do all the things. You just need to start with one.

Step 1: Identify your family's core values.

- What emotional skills do you want your child to grow up with?

Examples:
- Resilience
- Self-compassion
- Confidence
- Curiosity
- Kindness

How do you want your child to describe their relationship with you when they're older?

Step 2: Choose small, consistent practices.
Pick one or two practices from this workbook to begin with. Keep it simple and sustainable.

Examples:
- A daily affirmation at bedtime
- A weekly "feelings check-in" during dinner or before bed
- Practicing co-regulation by pausing to breathe together when things get heated
- Reading a story and talking about the characters' feelings

Step 3: Be flexible and adjust as needed.
Emotional growth is not linear. What works now may shift as your child grows. Keep checking in with yourself and your child. Stay curious. Stay flexible.

Action step:
Write down one small, realistic change you will implement this week to support your child's emotional growth.

Supporting Yourself as a Parent

You cannot pour from an empty cup. You cannot model self-regulation if your nervous system is frayed. Just as your child deserves emotional care, so do you.

Signs you may need more support:
- Feeling overwhelmed by your child's emotions.
- Reacting with more frustration or impatience than usual.
- Avoiding or forgetting the strategies in this book because you're emotionally exhausted.

Self-care ideas for parents:
- Give yourself permission to take breaks and set boundaries.
- Seek connection–friends, therapy, support groups.
- Use your own affirmations: "I am enough." "I'm learning, too."
- Celebrate small wins. A deep breath counts. So does showing up after a hard moment.

Journaling prompt:

What is one way I can support myself emotionally this week? How can I show up for myself with the same care I offer my child?

The Parenting Journey Continues

This is not the end. It's a beginning—a new chapter in how you show up for your child and for yourself. Some days will be easier than others. Some will be messy. But through it all, your commitment to emotional awareness, connection, and growth will leave a lasting impact.

Whenever you feel unsure, return to these questions:

- Am I seeing my child's emotions as valuable?
- Am I offering connection before correction?
- Am I allowing myself grace as I learn alongside my child?

This work isn't just about emotional literacy—it's about legacy. You're not just raising a child. You're shaping the next generation of emotionally grounded humans. And you're not doing it alone.

Key takeaways:

- Which practice from this book will I carry forward into my daily life?
- What is one thing I want to remember about parenting with emotional awareness?

♥ Thank you for showing up. For your child. For yourself. For the world you're helping shape through every moment of connection. You're exactly where you need to be.

Acknowledgments

To the parents, caregivers, teachers, therapists, grandparents, and big-hearted humans who picked up this workbook and said, "I want to do this differently," this is for you.

Thank you for choosing presence over perfection. For staying curious even when it would be easier to shut down. For pausing in the middle of the chaos to reflect, repair, and try again. We know how hard that is. And we know it matters.

You are the reason this work exists. You're the reason we kept writing when our own houses were messy, when we were running on little sleep and a lot of feelings. Your stories, your questions, your honesty, and vulnerability have helped us shape Slumberkins as it exists today, including the pages of this workbook.

We created *All Feelings Welcome* and this companion workbook because we believe deeply in your power. Not to control every moment (because, let's be real, toddlers with banana-covered hands are running the show), but to lead with love and connection, and to grow alongside your child in a way that transforms both of you.

To our SlumberFam community, you've shared your journeys, your wins, your hard moments, and your hilarious parenting fails with us. You've come together and created something bigger than we ever imagined. Your courage to do the inner work, even when it's messy or slow or uncomfortable, is what gives this movement meaning.

And if you're just joining us, welcome. There's a seat here for you too. No prep required. Just bring your heart.

This work is about connection. And we're so honored to be connected to you.

With love,

Callie + Kelly

About the Authors

Kelly Oriard and **Callie Christensen** are the co-authors of *All Feelings Welcome* and co-founders of Slumberkins, the leading emotional wellness brand for children. Their shared mission? To empower families with tools that support emotional growth—not just for kids, but for the adults guiding them too.

Callie Christensen is a former special education teacher turned chief brand officer, creative visionary, and story-shaper at Slumberkins. With a master's in teaching and real-world experience supporting students with intensive emotional needs, Callie brings compassion, practicality, and playfulness to everything she creates. As a mom, she's all too familiar with the messiness of parenting—and brings a healthy dose of humor and heart to the journey.

Kelly Oriard is a licensed family therapist, school counselor, and Slumberkins' chief therapeutic officer. With dual master's degrees in marriage and family therapy and in school counseling, she's spent her career supporting families, both in the therapy room and in classrooms. She's passionate about helping parents understand how their own emotional stories shape the way they show up—and how to rewrite those stories with intention.

Together, Kelly and Callie have authored over 50 books across the Slumberkins library, built a beloved line of cuddly creatures that help kids connect with their grownups and express their feelings, and co-executive produced the Emmy-nominated Slumberkins series on Apple TV+. Through it all, they remain moms first—figuring it out one bedtime meltdown at a time, just like you.

You can learn more at Slumberkins.com or find their daily doses of real talk and parenting support on Instagram @slumberkins.

Index